COMMUNITY LITERACIES AS SHARED RESOURCES FOR TRANSFORMATION

Through multiple narratives reflecting the complexity of participatory action research partnerships for social justice, this book sheds light on the dialogic spaces that intentionally support community literacies and rhetorical practices for inquiry and change. Applying literacy as social practice, Larson and Moses tell a story of a unique collaboration between community members and university faculty and students, who together transformed an urban corner store into a cornerstone of the community. Building on the emerging field of community literacies, the book captures the group's active work on the ground and, on another level, how transformation occurred in the dialogic spaces of the research team as it learned to embrace distributed expertise and multiple identities.

Joanne Larson is the Michael W. Scandling Professor of Education at the University of Rochester, USA.

George H. Moses is the Executive Director of North East Area Development, Inc. (NEAD) and Group 14621 Community Association in Rochester, USA.

EXPANDING LITERACIES IN EDUCATION
Jennifer Rowsell and Cynthia Lewis, Series Editors

Larson & Moses • *Community Literacies as Shared Resources for Transformation*

Rogers • *Reclaiming Powerful Literacies: New Horizons for Critical Discourse Analysis*

Zaidi & Rowsell, Eds. • *Literacy Lives in Transcultural Times*

Nordquist • *Literacy and Mobility: Complexity, Uncertainty and Agency at the Nexus of High School and College*

Comber • *Literacy, Place, and Pedagogies of Possibility*

Orellana • *Immigrant Children in Transcultural Spaces: Language, Learning and Love*

Enriquez, Johnson, Kontovourki, & Mallozzi, Eds. • *Literacies, Learning, and the Body: Putting Theory and Research into Pedagogical Practice*

Compton-Lilly • *Reading Students' Lives: Literacy Learning Across Time*

Visit www.routledge.com/education for additional information on titles in Expanding Literacies in Education.

COMMUNITY LITERACIES AS SHARED RESOURCES FOR TRANSFORMATION

Edited by Joanne Larson and George H. Moses

NEW YORK AND LONDON

First published 2018
by Routledge
711 Third Avenue, New York, NY 10017

and by Routledge
2 Park Square, Milton Park, Abingdon, Oxon OX14 4RN

Routledge is an imprint of the Taylor & Francis Group, an informa business

© 2018 Taylor & Francis

The right of Joanne Larson and George H. Moses to be identified as the authors of the editorial material, and of the authors for their individual chapters, has been asserted in accordance with sections 77 and 78 of the Copyright, Designs and Patents Act 1988.

All rights reserved. No part of this book may be reprinted or reproduced or utilized in any form or by any electronic, mechanical, or other means, now known or hereafter invented, including photocopying and recording, or in any information storage or retrieval system, without permission in writing from the publishers.

Trademark notice: Product or corporate names may be trademarks or registered trademarks, and are used only for identification and explanation without intent to infringe.

Library of Congress Cataloging-in-Publication Data
A catalog record for this book has been requested

ISBN: 978-1-138-24337-8 (hbk)
ISBN: 978-1-138-24339-2 (pbk)
ISBN: 978-1-315-27731-8 (ebk)

Typeset in Bembo
by Book Now Ltd, London

We dedicate this book to Miss Vera Mae Gilchrist, who first told us that it's all about family, relationships, and community.

CONTENTS

Our Research Team's Statement of Unity of Values in Unpredictable Times ix
   George Moses, Joanne Larson, Joyce Duckles,
   Joel Gallegos Greenwich, Robert Moses, Ryan Van Alstyne,
   Courtney Hanny, Jeremy Smith
Preface xi
Acknowledgments xiii

1   Introduction: History in the Present   1
    Joanne Larson, George Moses, Wallace Smith,
    Joel Gallegos Greenwich

2   Constructing Our Interdependence Model   20
    Joanne Larson, Courtney Hanny, Joyce Duckles,
    Joel Gallegos Greenwich, Robert Moses, George Moses,
    Kimberly Jones, Jeremy Smith

3   When Theory Met Practice: Methodology in the Versus   35
    Courtney Hanny, Joyce Duckles, Jeremy Smith, Robert Moses,
    Joel Gallegos Greenwich

4   Freedom Ain't Free … But It's Worth the Cost   54
    George Moses, Ryan Van Alstyne, Jeremy Smith, Joanne Larson,
    Brittany Calvin

5 We Are "All the Way Live": Reading Community   64
   Joanne Larson, Joel Gallegos Greenwich, George Moses,
   Robert Moses, Wallace Smith

6 Living Up to the Promise: School Connections   79
   Jeremy Smith, Joyce Duckles, Joanne Larson, Robert Moses

7 Doing Double Dutch: Rhythms of Transformation
   Across and Within the Community   104
   Joyce Duckles, George Moses, Ryan Van Alstyne

Index   *118*

OUR RESEARCH TEAM'S STATEMENT OF UNITY OF VALUES IN UNPREDICTABLE TIMES

George Moses, Joanne Larson, Joyce Duckles, Joel Gallegos Greenwich, Robert Moses, Ryan Van Alstyne, Courtney Hanny, Jeremy Smith

As a team, we are very aware of the time and place in which we are writing this book. We are not going to pretend we aren't working in unpredictable times; our sociohistorical theoretical lens makes it impossible for us to ignore what is happening. Our research team meetings are permeated with stories of fear and danger we hear from Beechwood residents. Some of us leave meetings to go to protests. We are committed to talk about the issues, rather than call out specific groups, and to focus on how these times have impacted the community in which we work. We stand together to provide leadership in tumultuous times by showing how people in these communities take a stand—we are not victims.

Other than the indigenous peoples of the Americas, all U.S. citizens have come from other countries. Our own personal family histories bring together stories from countries around the world. We are Christian and Jewish; we are male and female, straight, gay, and intersexed; we are black, white, and brown. The work of dialogue across difference is difficult work. We do this work in our collaboration described in this book. It is not simply about agreeing to disagree, it is about continuing to discuss the difficult, no matter what and while committing to each other as humans and as family. We stand together in this historical moment to do the work necessary to ensure that all humans are treated as such.

PREFACE

This book has multiple purposes. The first is to share the story of our work with a range of audiences so that authentic, collaborative community transformation can be shared more broadly. To this end, we employ stories. Using stories as the organizing principle throughout the book reflects how African Americans share and transmit history. This focus is in line with another key concept we use, that of sankofa. Sankofa refers to a Twi word from Ghana symbolizing looking to the past to frame the future. In a very real sense, these stories are the shared resources for community transformation we point to in the title of this book.

A second key purpose of this book is to reconsider what counts as knowledge and research. We argue that limiting research and knowledge production to the academy dramatically reduces what humans can learn about ourselves and our world. By collaborating with community in authentic ways, what we learn, and how we learn it, expands in unexpected ways that, in turn, build knowledge that would not have been possible without the collaboration. A third purpose follows from this one: to challenge the academy to value collaborative activist work. Currently, the academy values and rewards traditional, mostly experimental or quantitative, research that is published in tier-one, peer-reviewed research journals. This is important work that should be valued. What we argue is that collaborative, activist work in community be valued and rewarded in similar ways and not marginalized as "only" activism.

Each chapter begins with a story relevant to that chapter's focus. Chapter 1 gives a historical overview of activism in Rochester, and introduces our research team. Chapter 2 explains our Interdependence Model as a framework for understanding comprehensive community transformation. Chapter 3 ostensibly explains our research methods, but also discusses in depth how we came to be a trusting community of co-researchers, co-authors, and co-implementers.

Chapter 4 begins a series of chapters that discuss the various places and spaces in our Interdependence Model by telling the story of Rochester's Freedom School. Chapter 5 tells the story of a central place in our model, the Freedom Market. Chapter 6 shows how we have branched out to local schools as part of our community transformation work. Chapter 7 takes us into the future as we explain recent thinking that expands our model. We also offer some lessons learned that other communities may find helpful.

We write this book to community-based organizations, university-based researchers, faculty who teach research methods, community members, educators at all levels, and policy makers. We used a story trope and less formal academic language purposefully to be as inclusive as possible of this wide variety of audiences.

ACKNOWLEDGMENTS

We all want to thank Cynthia Lewis and Jennifer Rowsell for believing in the work we do and for supporting us to write this book. Most of all, we thank the people of Beechwood who opened their lives, their doors, and their community to us for years. We hope this book honors how much they shared with us.

1

INTRODUCTION

History in the Present

Joanne Larson, George Moses, Wallace Smith, Joel Gallegos Greenwich

> If there is no struggle, there is no progress.
> —*Frederick Douglass*, West India Emancipation Speech, *1857*

> Failure is impossible.
> —*Susan B. Anthony, as cited in Sherr, 1995*

Introduction

Once upon a time there was a little corner store in an urban neighborhood devastated by poverty...

Wait, that's not how you are supposed to open an academic book. Furthermore, that wouldn't be how you would start a story about the neighborhood we describe in this book. This book uses story as the main narrative trope, but the story is about collective agency and community transformation rather than devastation in the Beechwood neighborhood of Rochester, NY. The story we tell is about how different people, spaces, places, histories, and literacies came together to produce sustainable social, cultural, political, economic, and educational change. It is a story about relationships and how crucial they are to effecting any kind of change. Specifically, this story revolves around a robust, long-term partnership between the University of Rochester and residents of the Beechwood neighborhood. We are a collaborative research team made up of community residents/organizers in Beechwood, university researchers, and graduate students. We have come to call each other co-researchers, co-implementers, and co-authors as we seek to share what we learn every day with a broader audience.

From our perspective, there is no "exit strategy," as researchers often call the end of a study. There is no end to this work; we are friends and co-activists for life. We tell this story together in an edited volume format and through multiple narratives to account for the complexity of participatory action research partnerships for justice.

While our story is embedded in the broader historical context of Rochester (we get to that later in this chapter), we "start" the telling in the fall of 2011, when a group of community organizers at North East Area Development (NEAD), a community development organization in the Beechwood neighborhood, purchased an urban corner store across the street from their building. With this purchase, NEAD began an exciting entrepreneurial venture, rooted in an explicit social justice mission. George, NEAD's executive director and co-editor of this volume, reached out to Joanne (co-editor), given they had known each other since 2006 when they partnered in a separate research project. NEAD secured critical funding from the Greater Rochester Health Foundation, Farash Foundation, and the City of Rochester to support the research and the transformation of the corner store into the Freedom Market. We want to acknowledge the risk these funders took in supporting a project conceived of and implemented by community residents. George and NEAD staff wanted to begin a participatory ethnographic project to document the processes of change that they predicted would take shape through their work at this urban corner store. Based on a shared history of having been exploited or let down by university researchers or well-intentioned funders, NEAD staff were determined to collect their own evidence—to research rather than be researched. They were long tired of the steady stream of researchers or nonprofits with grants who sought to rescue their community. Grants ended and people left with no evidence of change in the neighborhood's circumstances (Larson et al., 2017).

Therefore, our unique collaboration was formed to document the processes that sought to transform a typical corner store into the cornerstone of its community—the Freedom Market. This would be the first corner store owned and operated by African Americans living in Beechwood (a neighborhood with 63% African American residents and 94 corner stores). In a neighborhood described as a "food desert," our initial ethnographic interest was supporting and documenting the shifts in food and health practices of the community with renewed access to nutritious alternatives. What took shape—what the community partners foresaw—was the co-construction of a unique dialogic space that created much more than access to food. What we did not foresee was the momentum for transformation across the community that would grow from these initial seeds of change. It soon became clear that the Freedom Market was only one node within a growing, grassroots network of justice initiatives connected to NEAD. Thus, it was only a matter of time before our research goal expanded from documenting change within the Freedom Market setting to also documenting the change occurring in and across other nodes in the community.

Our story, as told in this volume, is divided into seven chapters co-written by university and community members alike. In this chapter, we introduce our work and situate it within its broader theoretical and geopolitical context. In Chapter 2, we write about NEAD's growing network and share how we operate within and across these interdependent nodes. Specifically, we elaborate on our Interdependence Model which provides insight into a new and dynamic way of conceptualizing the community as a multi-nodal site for change, where new ways of being manifest in unique but connected ways. Chapter 3 is our methods chapter. We write about how we are intentionally crossing traditional disciplinary and cultural boundaries in the context of this university/community partnership—a partnership in which we often find and feel ourselves "living in the versus" as we recognize and address the contrary discourses necessary for authentic engagement and sustainable change. We share our thoughts on the dialogic space we've co-constructed over the years at the edge of our communities and how this space of dissensus (Ziarek, 2001) has come to be accepted and embraced by all on our research team—university and community team members alike. Chapter 4 tells the story of the Freedom School node, one of the first initiatives NEAD established as they began the work of community transformation in Beechwood. We describe how the Freedom School came about, what we have learned in the process, and how the Freedom School connects to all the spaces and places of our work. In Chapter 5, we go deeper into our work at the Freedom Market and discuss how generative frictions experienced within the store setting have played a key role in animating change. Chapter 6 describes how our network has grown to include work within local schools. Specifically, we document an evolving relationship with East High School. In its current iteration, we describe how the Freedom School has become an offsite option for struggling students as we partner with the University of Rochester in its new role as an Educational Partnership Organization (EPO). Finally, in Chapter 7, we write about how our multi-nodal approach has offered neighborhood residents increased access to community engagement opportunities and, in so doing, has fostered a fertile context in which new nodes might emerge.

Theoretical Context

As an overarching framework for this book, we use a definition of literacy as a social practice that is always embedded in contexts of use and relations of power (Larson & Marsh, 2015; Street, 1995). Seeing literacy as more than a set of autonomous skills afforded us the opportunity to understand how this community used a wide variety of literacy practices to accomplish transformative work. A simple documentation of the literacy practices would not suffice; we needed to understand how these practices were used and for what audiences and purposes. Building on Flower (2008, p. 7), we view community literacy as "a rhetorical action that calls forth a local public and creates a counterpublic structured around intercultural inquiry." Furthermore, the role of power relations and how they shifted during the course of the research is crucial to understanding the transformative work to which NEAD is committed.

In order to adequately account for the complexity and dynamism that became important in our data from early on, we drew from postmodern conceptualizations of knowledge production, identity, and change as dialogic democratic practices. Specifically, we employ the concepts of dialogicality and literacy as social practice (Bakhtin, 1981; Kinloch, 2005, 2009; Larson & Marsh, 2015; Marková, 2003; Rommetveit, 1991); the rhizomatic structure of interdependence and generativity (Deleuze & Guattari, 1987; Leander & Boldt, 2013; Leander & Rowe, 2006), and dissensus (Ziarek, 2001) as an ethical political model. That is, such a framework requires that we address difference and otherness being open to what we do not understand, what we are not familiar with—and at times, what we do not agree with. It is a different way of speaking and listening—crossing normative and discursive boundaries.

Adopting these perspectives allows us to move between interactional, spatial, and sociocritical frames fluidly, recognizing that they are interdependent and mutually constitutive. The idea that knowledge is distributed across people in everyday practices suggests that it is not "transmitted" linearly from one to another. Participants engaged in the authentic dialogical encounter (Bakhtin, 1981) or what Kinloch (2005) calls *democratic engagements*, do not send or give information to one another in a linear or unidirectional way, but create new meanings through engagement in the struggle to understand one another. Importantly, this interactional achievement, while *contractual* (Rommetveit, 1991), is not synthetic. That is, this sharedness is a temporary and partial sharedness—difference is not neutralized or blended in this model. Rather, self and other maintain their irreducible differences. As such, the work of dialogicality is messy and interminable—a site of struggle and friction, or what Emdin (2013) might refer to as the *pain* of history that must remain alive in order to fuel passion and action. In his view, the end of pain signals retreat from thinking and fighting—the death of passion, foreclosing change. That's the sort of passion that fuels our desire to tell this story. We use this framework to understand both the interactional processes in and around the Market and our research team meetings as we talk across differences of position and ideology.

Our story and our work build upon and contribute to the growing field of community literacies (Cammarota, 2011; Flower, 2008; Kinloch, 2005, 2009; Pahl & Burnett, 2013) as practices that challenge the status quo by engaging in collaborative processes of dialogue and critical inquiry. We conceptualize the nodes within NEAD's network as spaces and places for bringing new social futures into dialogue and co-creating opportunities to take part in a new rhetoric of public engagement. We hold that the power of these spaces and places can best be experienced across the community through observing patterns of engagement and community literacy practices. Mackey (2010) connects the importance of place with literacy practices. As we read, we take the "space" of the letters and words of a book and turn them into the "place of our own reading, invested with our understanding of the world" (p. 331). Interpretation, meaning making, and subjectivities emerge from a growing understanding of the world and our places within it, and these embodied experiences lead to "embedded literacies" (p. 329) that build connections between our everyday lives and the literacy practices that lead to change. Declaring that traditional critique with a vision of social, political, and spiritual transformation requires "even more" of researchers, Flower (2008) summarizes the challenges, power, and privileges of this iterative and collaborative work on the ground:

> The effort to discover and describe, to enact and revise what a *transformative more* could be is one of the most energetically exploratory agendas to emerge in our field ... What these experiments seek is a way to conduct a clear-eyed, historically grounded, intellectually rigorous *critique* of others and ourselves and at the same time to imagine and act on a *vision of transformation*. Such a vision would draw us by its rich articulation of possibility, its self-critical negotiation with experience, and its feet-on-the-ground willingness to act, revise, and act again.
>
> *(pp. 1–2, italics in original)*

As we have developed our Interdependence Model following Massey (1994), we define place as "porous networks of social relations" (p. 121) in which geography matters. In a very real sense, where Beechwood is, its geography, shapes outcomes such as life expectancy and educational attainment. Each node in our model is a place where social relations come together. Spaces are constructed between nodes and between people as we navigate across and within the geographies of Beechwood and Rochester.

Current studies of home and community literacies are extending the focus on space and place. Pahl and Burnett (2013) present an overview of the related strands in this field and call for interdisciplinary frameworks that include New Literacy Studies, multimodality, and ethnographic understandings of communities. The New Literacy Studies (NLS) of Barton and Hamilton (1998), Gee (2007), and Street (1993, 2000) brought attention to context and the situated nature of literacy practice. Using primarily ethnographic methods, studies in urban literacies (e.g. Kinloch, 2010) have considered geographic as well as sociocultural factors shaping literacy practices. Others (e.g. Gee, 2004; Moll, 2000) have proposed more fluid and multimodal notions of literacy across contexts. Studies are also demonstrating the ways literacies are "materialized" across home and community settings. They become more difficult to recognize and document because they are "linked across invisible lines to other spaces and contexts" (Pahl & Burnett, 2013, p. 8). Following scholars who discuss the spatial turn in literacy studies, we tell the story of the various, fluid spaces that community members and university researchers travel and how literacy shapes and is shaped by those spaces.

This focus on movement and connections directs our attention to pathways, boundaries, and edges. Such attention is echoed in studies of urban places and the ways that they are conceptualized. Lynch (1960) proposed that people create mental images of their cities through pathways, nodes, districts, landmarks, and edges. Lefebvre (1991) reminds us that spaces are not fixed; they are always under construction. Drawing on critical geography, we document the processes of one community's attempt to take back the city (Lefebvre, 1991) and access what Soja (2010) refers to as urban residents' spatial rights. More recently, the work by Ito and colleagues (2013) on connected learning is adopting a metaphor of movement to capture their views of learning and education as "a much more flexible and networked enterprise that happens as part of participation in diverse forms of culture and community" (p. 34).

As we have come to see the spaces between places as linked in multiple ways, we are rethinking literacy practices as involving flows and shifts. As researchers, this means paying attention to "lost things, traveling, inscriptions, lines and traces, street literacies and oral stories, in short the complex, meshed 'stuff' of everyday cultural life" (Miller, 2010 as referenced in Pahl & Burnett, 2013, p. 9). We argue that these pathways highlight the power of boundary crossings. We find dialogic encounters and democratic engagement fostered in spaces of connection and interaction, and in particular those that work across difference. An early insight of our research team when we analyzed data was that it was all the same people working across different spaces and places in the neighborhood and, more broadly, the city of Rochester. This "aha" prompted a vibrant discussion of what those spaces and places were that eventually became our Interdependence Model (see Figure 2.2 in Chapter 2). As Burbules (2004) suggests:

> A place is a socially or subjectively meaningful space. It has an objective, locational dimension: people can look for a place, find it, move within it. But it also means something important to a person or a group of people, and this latter, more subjective, dimension may or may not be communicable to others. When people are in a place, they know where they are and what it means to be there.
>
> (p. 174)

Together, we sought to explore these meanings. We write about how dialogic spaces are being co-constructed in everyday interactions that intentionally support community literacies and rhetorical practices for inquiry and change (Flower, 2008). This volume embodies the momentum of these practices and these spaces and captures our active work on the ground. At another level, transformation occurs in the dialogic spaces of our research team where we have learned to embrace distributed expertise and multiple identities. Participation in these spaces captures our move toward dissensus (Ziarek, 2001) as a practice to challenge stagnation and the building of relationships across difference based on trust and our shared passion for justice. We begin to answer Flower's (2008) call for "a revisable image of transformation" (p. 2). Throughout this book, we present the many ways we have acted, revised, and acted again. To ground the volume, below we present a brief history of Rochester and its activist past.

Community members on our research team added the principles of *nguzo saba* to our theoretical lens. The seven principles of *nguzo saba*—unity, self-determination, collective work and responsibility, cooperative economics, purpose, creativity, and faith—were developed by Maulana Karenga as the foundation for the African American celebration of Kwanzaa, which focuses on honoring African American heritage.[1] *Umoja* (unity) focuses on building unity across family, community, nation and race; *kujichagulia* (self-determination) emphasizes the rights of the people to define, name, create, and speak for themselves; *ujima* (collective work and responsibility) works toward collaborative problem-solving among community members; *ujamaa* (cooperative economics) states that the community needs to own its own stores and benefit together from the economics generated; *nia* (purpose) focuses on collective actions that would bring the community back to its original greatness; *kuumba* (creativity) argues that the work of the community must always be to make their spaces more beautiful than they were; and, *imani* (faith) emphasizes the community's belief in itself and each other and in the righteousness of their collective struggle. Each of these principles can be seen in the work described in this book. For example, our co-authorship of this volume speaks to self-determination or the ability to determine what is said about our work and how it is said.

Furthermore, we use the concept of sankofa to reflect our process of looking back to history to frame the present and the future. Sankofa is a term used by the Akan people of West Africa that means to go back to a community's roots to move forward. Sankofa is represented as a mythic bird that typically has an egg on its back which symbolizes the future.[2] As Ryan puts it, "it's basically going back and gettin' it." We will discuss more about how the image of the sankofa bird is used in a series of murals we have painted in the neighborhood in Chapter 2 (Larson et al., 2017).

History of Activism in Rochester

Our activist work does not begin in a vacuum, nor is a focus on social justice new to Rochester. The following section outlines Rochester's history, focusing specifically on its history of activism and social justice work. To begin, we honor Frederick Douglass as the narrative link in this introductory chapter. Douglass (1845) tells the story of when he realized he was free as follows:

> This battle with Mr. Covey was the turning point in my career as a slave. It rekindled the few expiring embers of freedom, and revived within me a sense of my own manhood. It recalled the departed self-confidence,

and inspired me again with a determination to be free. The gratification afforded by the triumph was a full compensation for whatever else might follow, even death itself. He only can understand the deep satisfaction which I experienced, who has himself repelled by force the bloody arm of slavery. I felt as I never felt before. It was a glorious resurrection, from the tomb of slavery, to the heaven of freedom. My long-crushed spirit rose, cowardice departed, bold defiance took its place; and I now resolved that, however long I might remain a slave in form, the day had passed forever when I could be a slave in fact. I did not hesitate to let it be known of me, that the white man who expected to succeed in whipping, must also succeed in killing me.

(pp. 72–73)

His pursuit of freedom continues today for the residents of Beechwood. Through our use of the sankofa metaphor, we look back to Douglass's work to inform the work we do today and in the future.

Early History and Activism

Foucault (1982) has challenged notions of the linear historical narrative in his analysis of human knowledge production. In this work, he argues that there is no history per se, but that history only exists in the present. We use this understanding that history both shapes and is shaped by the present (that it does not exist outside of being invoked in the present) to locate our collaborative work in Rochester, NY. We are not starting from scratch in our activist work. Rochester has a deep history of radical activism upon which we build. Susan B. Anthony and Frederick Douglass both worked in Rochester to change lives for women and African Americans in ways that foreshadowed activist work over time in Rochester, some of which we discuss in this book. Their history is present in our work as we seek to change the conditions in the Beechwood neighborhood. Susan B. Anthony's last spoken words before her death, "failure is impossible," guide our work.

We begin our historical narrative in this chapter by acknowledging and offering gratitude to the Iroquois Nation. They were the first people on the land that is now Rochester. Jesuit missionaries made first contact with the Seneca nation[3] in the 17th century, followed by Western European farmers. Rochester, named after Nathaniel Rochester, quickly moved from village in 1703 to town in 1788. By 1888, George Eastman invented the Kodak camera, establishing Kodak as a corporation and Rochester as a center of innovation and manufacturing. Kodak would go on to become a significant employer in the region. By the 1950s, Rochester's economy was booming with industrial expansions by Kodak, IBM, Bausch and Lomb, and Xerox; however, as the discussion below of the 1964 riots shows, exclusionary hiring practices activated resistance.

With the decline of these companies in the 2000s, the University of Rochester is now the largest employer, following larger national shifts toward a knowledge economy (Gee, Hull, & Lankshear, 1996).

The 1950s also saw an increase in African American and Latinx[4] immigration due to manufacturing jobs at these corporations and the resulting promise of careers. However, racialized hiring practices led to discrimination and poverty in these populations. Building on the long tradition of social activism in Rochester and the social movements of the 1960s, the race riots that began in July 1964 represent a significant shift in the population and economics of Rochester. White flight (as the exodus of White families from the inner-city areas is known) began to form an outer ring of suburbs as earlier Europeans were replaced by the influx of African Americans from the south and Latinx from Puerto Rico and other Caribbean nations.

Alongside these fluid migrations, Rochester was home to significant social activism based on civil and human rights issues. Susan B. Anthony and Frederick

FIGURE 1.1 Susan B. Anthony and Elizabeth Cady Stanton (Sarony, 1896)

Douglass were both resident in Rochester during their work to change lives for slaves and women. Rochester is considered the birthplace of the women's movement in Seneca Falls. Even today, women recognize Anthony on election day by pasting their "I voted" stickers on her gravestone.

We believe it is important to know that the route to women's freedom and success in modern society was inspired centuries ago by the Seneca Mothers of the Haudenosaunee (the Iroquois Confederacy), whose people occupied the Rochester region. Their matriarchal society and decision-making powers determined marriage arrangements, property ownership, clan membership and tribal identification, and tribal leadership. Building on the Seneca matriarchal society as inspiration, Susan B. Anthony and her colleagues (Elizabeth Cady Stanton, Jane Hunt, Mary Ann M'Clintock, Lucretia Mott, and Martha Wright)

FIGURE 1.2 Frederick Douglass (Legg, 1879)

presented the Declaration of Sentiments at the first Women's Rights Convention in Seneca Falls, NY.[5] Frederick Douglass was the only African American to attend this convention.

Settling in Rochester in 1848, Frederick Douglass began publishing his first abolitionist newspaper, *The North Star*, from the basement of the Memorial AME Zion Church. His use of literacy as a transformative tool foreshadows our own justice-driven research on community literacies in the Beechwood community. His publication of *The North Star* continued to put him in a prominent place locally and nationally. His collaboration with Anthony reached a breaking point over a disagreement on whether initiatives for black male suffrage would overshadow women's rights. Douglass was able to build relationships with other activists in the area, such as Sojourner Truth and Harriet Tubman in their work on the Underground Railroad as it passed through Rochester.

It is with respect to these pillars of human rights activists that we continue the work to bring justice to African American, Latinx, and other historically marginalized communities in Rochester. Moving forward in our story, we come to a pivotal moment in Rochester's history in which Wallace Smith, one of the authors of this chapter, was a key leader. The story of the 1964 riots that follows was adapted from a story told by "Uncle" Wallace at a research team meeting in 2015.

Local Uprising

Part of the African American culture in the 1960s was to have street dances every weekend. While intended as celebratory by residents, police responded by picking people out randomly and beating them. On July 24, 1964 at the corner of Ward and Joseph Avenues, the crowd turned on the police who brought dogs to control them. Conversations about police brutality had begun around the same time due to the beating of Rufus Fairwell, a well-known local store owner. Given tensions between African Americans and the police were already high, July 24 became the breaking point. People began breaking into businesses and taking things; the Hanover Houses housing project erupted and people spilled out into the streets. The violence lasted about a week. At one point, the police chief came to try to talk to rioters, but the crowd turned his car over. A local community activist, Mildred Johnson, tried to calm the crowd, to no avail. As the violence spread from the East side of Rochester to the West side, local people tried to pull together community leaders to calm them down. However, these community leaders did not have any real handle on street people. Churches got involved, who in turn sent for Saul Alinsky to do some organizing. Fight Independence God Honor Today (FIGHT) grew out of the work with Alinsky. By the time the dust from the uprising settled, four people had been killed, 350 injured, 1,000 arrested, and over 204 stores looted or damaged.

TABLE 1.1 Demographic shifts

Racial composition	2010	1990	1970	1940
White	43.7%	61.1%	82.4%	97.6%
—Non-Hispanic	37.6%	58.3%	80.2%	n.a.
Black or African American	41.7%	31.5%	16.8%	2.3%
Hispanic or Latinx (of any race)	16.4%	8.7%	2.8%	n.a.
Asian	3.1%	1.8%	0.2%	n.a.

Wallace Smith, a key member of our research team and a daily presence at the Freedom Market, has a long history of working toward social justice, beginning in the 1960s when he served as the president of FIGHT. FIGHT's main purpose was to serve as a voice for the impoverished Black community of Rochester. In one of their most notable and daring undertakings, FIGHT protested against Eastman Kodak for neglecting the Black community in its training and hiring practices, which resulted in an increase in the hiring and training of Black employees at Eastman. Wallace was the fifth and last president of this organization in 1976.

After the riots, the status quo was shaken and government leaders had lost touch with people in the community. At the time, the Beechwood neighborhood was predominantly White and staunchly prejudiced. Wallace remembers being called names and having frequent negative interactions as Blacks moved in "pockets" to and from school. Beechwood's demographics began to change as Whites moved to the suburbs. Since the 1960s, Rochester's African American population has more than doubled in size, and neighborhoods like Beechwood have become predominantly African American (see Table 1.1).

Modern Rochester

According to the 2010 census,[6] the city's population was 43.7% White or White American, 41.7% Black, 0.5% American Indian and Alaska Native, 3.1% Asian, 0.0% Native Hawaiian and Other Pacific Islander, 6.6% from some other race and 4.4% from two or more races. Some 16.4% of the total population were Hispanic or Latinx of any race, mostly made up of Puerto Ricans. Non-Hispanic Whites accounted for 37.6% of the population in 2010, compared to 80.2% in 1970.

Over the course of the past 50 years, Rochester has become a major center for immigration and a resettlement city for refugees, particularly for arrivals from Eastern Europe and Southeastern Europe, sub-Saharan Africa, Bosnia, Nepal, Syria, and the Caribbean. Rochester has the highest percentage of Puerto Ricans of any major city in the United States, one of the four largest Turkish American communities, one of the largest Jamaican American communities in any major U.S. city, and a large concentration of Polish Americans, along with nearby Buffalo, NY. In 1997, Rochester had the largest per capita deaf population in the United States. This is attributed to the fact that it is home to the National Technical Institute for the Deaf.

It is within this broader context that our collaboration operates. We are indebted to those who preceded us as we build upon the rich history of justice work in Rochester. Our work reflects our previously described commitment to the seven principles of *nguzo saba* which guide all the work we do in the community and have played a key role our in collaborative data analysis and the construction of our Interdependence Model (described in Chapter 2). Our research team makes up the "cast of characters" who narrate their stories in this book. While the list of research team members has changed over the years of our Freedom Market collaboration (now in its sixth year), Table 1.2 below lists the researchers who have participated from the beginning and contributed to the authoring of this book.

Many university doctoral and masters students and community members also contributed greatly to the research and knowledge-building processes. We acknowledge them here and thank them for their hard work: Dr. Tomás Boatwright, Shirley Boone, Maurice Brooks, Eric Meyer, Hoang Pham, TaShara Smalls, Brandon Stroud, Van White, Xiaoxue "Archer" Wu, Emmah Mutezo, and Christie Weidenhamer.

We have structured this book around storytelling practices in the Beechwood community. Each chapter focuses on a story that features a "character" or characters from our team. In the paragraphs that follow, we introduce the cast of characters in more detail so that readers can know who we are and make a choice to follow one or more of us through the stories we tell. Each of us has a

TABLE 1.2 The market research team

Name	Role	Race/ethnicity
Brittany Calvin	Freedom School/resident	Black/African American
Joyce Duckles	Warner faculty/co-principal investigator	White/Jewish
Joel Gallegos Greenwich	Warner doctoral student/resident	White/Brazilian American
Courtney Hanny	Warner doctoral student	White/European
Joanne Larson	Warner faculty/principal investigator	White/European
George Moses	Executive Director NEAD/resident	Black/African American
Robert Moses	NEAD/resident	Black/African American
Kim Nelson	NEAD/resident	Black/African American
Jeremy Smith	Freedom School/resident	Black/African American
Wallace Smith	Freedom Market/resident	Black/African American
Ryan Van Alstyne	Freedom School	Black/African American

nickname given by different group members that captures an attribute the group cherishes. This naming practice is rooted in *kujichagulia*—the self-determination principle of *nguzo saba*—in which we name and define ourselves. After Joanne and George, our brief bios are organized chronologically, based on when each person joined the team.

The Cast of Characters

Joanne "Joanie loves Chachi" Larson: Joanne is the Michael W. Scandling Professor of education at the University of Rochester's Warner Graduate School of Education and Human Development. She met George Moses in 2006 when she was doing an ethnography of an earlier community transformation initiative. We connected well around our commitment to justice work and began a friendship and research partnership that continues to this day. For the Freedom Market project, Joanne was the official principal investigator on a grant from the Greater Rochester Health Foundation to conduct ethnography of the Freedom Market project. She was given the nickname "Joanie loves Chachi" by George because of the way she branches off yet stays connected to this group, like a sitcom spinoff.

George "Brother man from the 5th floor" Moses: George is the executive director of North East Area Development (NEAD), the Group 14621 neighborhood organization. He is a longtime resident of the Beechwood neighborhood and a well-respected leader in the African American community in Rochester. He proudly served in the United States Navy. During our work together, George was appointed by the mayor to serve as chair of the Rochester Housing Authority. He is committed to building capacity in his team as part of our goal of sustainability. If the work we do relies on the labor of one charismatic leader, it will fall apart after this person leaves. "Brother man from the 5th floor" explains George's omnipresence in the community, especially given his office is on the 2nd floor of the NEAD building and looks down at the Freedom Market's front door.

Robert "Schooly" Moses: Robert is the director of economic development for NEAD and the manager of the Freedom Market. He is a father of three and has lived in Beechwood for over 40 years. He got the nickname "Schooly" because he was a street scholar. This means his street credibility is "on fleek" due to his 40 plus years in the community.

Wallace "Uncle Ruckus" Smith: Wallace is a deeply respected elder in the community who is known for his tough love. Much of this book draws on his experience as a community activist in the 1960s, working with Saul Alinsky after the 1964 riots in Rochester. He is a special forces veteran, uncle, and grandfather—considered a father by many. Whether he is blood relation or not, he is uncle to everyone. He is a staunch advocate for civil rights in the African

American community, who will call out racism at every turn. The "Uncle Ruckus" nickname refers to his practice of calling out injustice, or causing a ruckus everywhere he goes.

Jeremy "Dassani" Smith: Jeremy grew up on the Eastside of Rochester and attended Rochester City School District's schools 52 and Frederick Douglass. When he reached 8th grade, coaches recognized his athletic ability and tried to get him a scholarship to a local private Catholic school. He didn't like that particular one, but he did end up attending another private Catholic school on full scholarship, graduating in 2004. He attended Alfred University but was dismissed because of academics. After some family troubles, he began to take school seriously to support his family. After attending Monroe Community College for two years, he transferred to St. John Fisher to study business management. He began working with children at NEAD in 2007 and slowly realized his calling was working with youth. Jeremy shifted his attention to teacher certification, which he received in 2015. Hence, his nickname of "Dassani" means "he's just like water, he flows through all obstacles."

Kimberly "Boondock minister" Nelson: Kim serves as a coordinator of NEAD's family and community engagement initiatives. She began her relationship with NEAD as a parent at Freedom School's summer program. Recognizing her clear expertise in parent advocacy and leadership, she was hired at NEAD. "Boondock minister" signifies her rural upbringing and her spiritual connection to the community.

Brittany "B-Cal" or "Ops" Calvin: Brittany serves as the operations manager (hence "Ops") at Freedom School. She came to NEAD as a volunteer from Monroe Community College and was inspired to give back to the community after seeing the Freedom School in action. Her nickname is a shortened pronunciation of her name and represents her power as a strong black woman.

Joyce "JD" Duckles: Joyce is clinical assistant professor in Counseling and Human Development at Warner. She has long focused her work on family engagement and community development through constructivist grounded theory and participatory research practices. She fit into the team immediately and passed George's trustworthiness test when she first met him at the American Educational Research Association annual meeting in Vancouver 2012. She is co-PI on the ethnography. She has deepened relationships with families in the neighborhood, specifically working along with local women and families to build a sustainable business of greenhouses and gardens to create access to fresh food, build social and economic pathways and support activism and change. Aside from being her initials, the nickname "JD" also refers to how the team asks her all the questions about Judaism. Some call her "Doc."

Courtney "Encyclopedia Brown" Hanny: Courtney earned her PhD from the University of Rochester's Warner Graduate School of Education and Human Development in 2016, and is now a Research Analyst at the State University New York (SUNY) Research Foundation. With a background in art education, literature, and alternative community literacies, her research employs a psychological anthropological approach to social difference, identity, and epistemological justice in learning contexts. She got her "Encyclopedia Brown" nickname because of her seemingly inexhaustible knowledge base; she could pull out a list of references or ideas at any moment.

Joel "Magic Man" Gallegos Greenwich: Joel is a PhD candidate at the University of Rochester's Warner Graduate School of Education and Human Development. He has served as a graduate research assistant on the Freedom Market project since 2012. His research revolves around understanding the perspectives and experiences of African American high school students who have been identified as "over-age and under-credited" and how they make sense of the opportunity gap in education. When not working on his dissertation, he enjoys performing magic as a means of building relational bridges in the community, leading to his nickname, "Magic Man."

Ryan "Brother Raheem" Van Alstyne: Ryan moved to Rochester in 1972 when he was four. He met George when they were both freshmen in high school in Rochester. Following the family legacy, Ryan began community activism in high school, serving as the youngest director of a not-for-profit when he volunteered to take over the summer program. Together with George, he was one of the founders of the Freedom School. His nickname, "Brother Raheem," means he has what it takes to get the job done.

Collaborative Writing With Community

So how in the world did we bring all these people together to actually write this book? It proved to be a significant challenge. The university people write for a living and share similar writing practices, such as brainstorming, creating outlines, sharing multiple drafts, and using track changes or a shared Google doc to revise. Community members communicated differently. They preferred to think together out loud, draw, read, and talk—practices that reflect their view of themselves as collaborative writers who have a shared history. After a few false starts, we hit on a process that worked for everyone. We created a shared Google folder where drafts were located and worked on by university folks, even though community members used it to read drafts on laptops or smartphones or to get them to print out. We met weekly to talk things through and different people wrote down what others said. Whiteboards were key in this process. As we talked, different people would rush up to the board to write something, draw lines between things, or to make exclamation points. Figure 1.3 is an example of one of these boards.

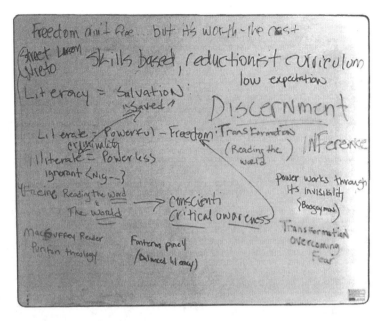

FIGURE 1.3 Brainstorming together

We are excited to share with readers of this book what we have accomplished and how we have accomplished it. We hope that our story inspires you in your own work and challenges you to consider how different people, spaces, histories, and literacies might come together to uniquely produce change in *your* community. After all, these desperate times require *all* of us to remain vigilant and engaged in grassroots activism.

Notes

1 See www.officialkwanzaawebsite.org/NguzoSaba.shtml for further details.
2 See www.sankofa.org/mission for more information.
3 The Seneca are one of the six nations of the Iroquois Confederacy. The other five are: Mohawk, Onondaga, Oneida, Cayuga, and Tuscarora.
4 We use the term Latinx to include gender identities beyond the masculine/feminine binary—see http://tinyurl.com/o7y5vrq.
5 See http://ecssba.rutgers.edu/docs/seneca.html for full details.
6 See www.census.gov/2010census/.

References

Bakhtin, M. (1981). *The dialogic imagination*. M. Holquist (Ed.), M. Holquist & C. Emerson (Trans.). Austin, TX: University of Texas Press.
Barton, D. & Hamilton, M. (1998). *Local literacies: Reading and writing in one community*. New York, NY: Routledge.

Burbules, N.C. (2004). Ways of thinking about educational quality. *Educational Researcher, 33*(6), 4–10.
Cammarota, J. (2011). From hopelessness to hope: Social justice pedagogy in urban education and youth development. *Urban Education, 46*(4), 828–844. DOI:10.1177/0042085911399931.
Deleuze, G. & Guattari, F. (1987). *A thousand plateaus: Capitalism and schizophrenia*. Minneapolis, MN: University of Minnesota Press.
Douglass, F. (1845/1995). *Narrative of the life of Frederick Douglass, an African slave. Written by himself*. Electronic Edition. Boston, MA: Anti-slavery Office. Retrieved 12/29/16 from http://docsouth.unc.edu/neh/douglass/douglass.html.
Douglass, F. (1857). *West India Emancipation Speech*. Canandaigua, NY.
Emdin, C. (2013). *Pedagogies for social change*. Keynote speech delivered at Hip-Hop Literacies Conference, The Ohio State University, Columbus, OH.
Flower, L. (2008). *Community literacy and the rhetoric of public engagement*. Carbondale, IL: SIU Press.
Foucault, M. (1982). *The archeology of knowledge*. New York, NY: Vintage.
Gee, J.P. (2004). *Situated language and learning: A critique of traditional schooling*. New York, NY: Routledge.
Gee, J.P. (2007). *Social linguistics and literacies*. New York, NY: Routledge.
Gee, J.P., Hull, G.A., & Lankshear, C. (1996). *The new work order: Behind the language of the new capitalism*. Boulder, CO: Westview Press.
Ito, M., Gutiérrez, K., Livingstone, S., Penuel, B., Rhodes, J., Salen, K., Schor, J., Sefton-Green, J., & Watkins, C.S. (2013). *Connected learning: An agenda for research and design*. Irvine, CA: Digital Media and Learning Research Hub.
Kinloch, V. (2005). Poetry, literacy, and creativity: Fostering effective learning strategies in an urban classroom. *English Education, 37*(2), 96–114.
Kinloch, V. (2009). Suspicious spatial distinctions literacy research with students across school and community contexts. *Written Communication, 26*(2), 154–182.
Kinloch, V. (2010). *Harlem on our minds: Place, race and the literacies of urban youth*. New York, NY: Teachers College Press.
Larson, J. & Marsh, J. (2015). *Making literacy real: Theories and practices for learning and teaching* (2nd ed.). London, UK: Sage.
Larson, J., Hanny, C., Duckles, J., Pham, H., & Moses, R. (2017). Expressing community through Freedom Market and visual connections. *Pedagogies: An International Journal, Special Issue*.
Leander, K. & Boldt, G. (2013). Rereading "A pedagogy of multiliteracies": Bodies, texts, and emergence. *Journal of Literacy Research, 45*(1), 22–46.
Leander, K. & Rowe, D. (2006). Mapping literacy spaces in motion: A rhizomatic analysis of a classroom literacy performance. *Reading Research Quarterly, 41*(4), 428–460.
Lefebvre, H. (1991). *The production of space*. D. Nicholson-Smith (Trans.). Oxford: Blackwell.
Legg, F.W. (1879). Frederick Douglass [online image]. Retrieved June 16, 2017 from the U.S. National Archives and Records Administration. Available at https://catalog.archives.gov/id/558770.
Lynch, K. (1960). *The image of the city*. Boston: MIT Press.
Mackey, M. (2010). Reading from the feet up: The local work of literacy. *Children's Literature in Education, 41*, 323–339. DOI:10.1007/s10583-010-9114-z.
Marková, I. (2003). *Dialogicality and self-representations: The dynamics of mind*. Cambridge, UK: Cambridge University Press.

Massey, D. (1994). *Space, place, and gender*. Cambridge, UK: Polity Press.
Moll, L. (2000). Inspired by Vygotsky: Ethnographic experiments in education. In C. Lee & P. Smagorinsky (Eds.), *Vygotskian perspectives on literacy research: Constructing meaning through collaborative inquiry* (pp. 256–268). Cambridge, UK: Cambridge University Press.
Pahl, K. & Burnett, K. (2013). Literacies in homes and communities. In B. Comber, T. Cremin, & K. Hall (Eds.), *International handbook of research on children's literacy, learning and culture* (1st ed.) (pp. 3–14). Somerset, NJ: John Wiley & Sons.
Rommetveit, R. (1991). On axiomatic features of a dialogic approach to language and mind. In I. Marková & K. Foppa, (Eds.), *The dynamics of dialogue*. New York, NY: Springer-Verlag.
Sarony, N. (1896). Elizabeth Cady Stantion and Susan B. Anthony [online image]. Retrieved June 16, 2017 from the National Portrait Gallery, Smithsonian Institution. Available at http://npg.si.edu/object/npg_S_NPG.77.48.
Sherr, L. (1995). *Failure is impossible: Susan B. Anthony in her own words*. New York, NY: Random House.
Soja, E. (2010). *Seeking spatial justice*. Minneapolis, MN: University of Minnesota Press.
Street, B. (ed.) (1993). *Cross-cultural approaches to literacy*. Cambridge, UK: Cambridge University Press.
Street, B. (1995). *Social Literacies: Critical Approaches to Literacy in Development, Ethnography, and Education*. London: Longman.
Street, B.V. (2000). Literacy events and literacy practices: Theory and practice in the new literacy studies. In M. Martin-Jones & K. Jones (Eds.), *Multilingual literacies: Reading and writing different worlds* (pp. 17–29). Philadelphia, PA: John Benjamins.
Ziarek, E.P. (2001). *An ethics of dissensus: Postmodernity, feminism, and the politics of radical democracy*. Stanford, CA: Stanford University Press.

2
CONSTRUCTING OUR INTERDEPENDENCE MODEL[1]

Joanne Larson, Courtney Hanny, Joyce Duckles, Joel Gallegos Greenwich, Robert Moses, George Moses, Kimberly Jones, Jeremy Smith

Introduction

Early in our research together, our research team realized that the very idea of "a research site" was misleading: we realized we were dealing with a network of places, spaces, persons, and interactions that functioned as an interdependent and dynamic network. The diagram in Figure 2.2 is the result of the research team's collaborative efforts to make sense or "read" these processes. But, like any schematic, its symmetry and organization need to be understood as the result of a textual representation of something that is far more complex and not static. The story of this model's production is not over, given we are constantly rethinking it; however, the moment we first drew it occurred at a research team meeting. We were all talking through different ideas when Courtney, in her role as Encyclopedia Brown, brought up the concept of rhizome as perhaps a conceptual way to think about what we were talking about. "What's a rhizome?" someone asked. Before she could explain, people started pulling out their phones to look it up. Quickly, George said, "Oh, we call that grassroots." With this connection, the word and concept of rhizome became part of our shared vocabulary. Shortly thereafter, George stood up and went up to the chart paper resting on an easel and started to draw nodes in our root system. Joanne also got up and started to draw connecting lines between the different nodes we found ourselves traveling across: Freedom School, Freedom Market, NEAD, the University of Rochester, the Beechwood neighborhood, and two different schools. Light bulbs starting going off for everyone. We realized we had hit on something that made sense. The photos shown in Figure 2.1 were taken that day.

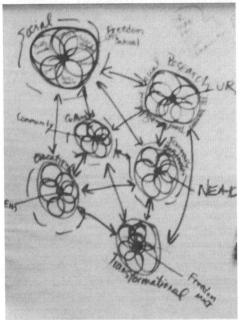

FIGURE 2.1 Making sense

The rhizome metaphor, based on the underground system of nodes, roots, and shoots, mirrors the ways in which surface entities that appear distinct and separate have complex subterranean connections (Deleuze & Guattari, 1987). A change in one entity affects multiple others in often unexpected ways, and new "shoots" can be generated at any time. Countering the arboreal model comprised of a central trunk, root, and branch system, the rhizomatic model eschews such a hierarchical structuring and relies upon a horizontal model. As Leander and Boldt (2013) and Leander and Rowe (2006) have demonstrated, the rhizome has proven a useful model for understanding the emergent, embodied and interconnected qualities of literacies in social lives.

Connecting to Literacy

We suggest that such an understanding mirrors the way in which "literacy" ought to be understood in this community context. That is, literacy needs to be seen as a set of multiple and changing social practices that carry and shift across specific sites and persons within a complex web of relations. In other words, to be "literate" or educated means negotiating these interdependencies and the challenges and conflicts that each implies. Rather than seeing challenges and conflicts as deficits, we posit that they are the fuel that enervates dynamism and change. We use our collaboratively developed schematic along with a compilation of vignettes from the ethnographic data to flesh out the possibilities and constraints that this Interdependence Model of literacy affords for understanding learning and social transformations.

Being literate, or "knowing how to read" these networked spaces invokes a set of practices that recognizes multiple, sometimes conflicting and overlapping, nodes of interdependence. Literacies flow through and within all these hubs of interdependence. The tensions, struggles, and "pain" (Emdin, 2013) involved serve to animate what would otherwise be a static map. In other words, what generates change are the authentic (and therefore often messy and contradictory) engaged interactions that take place between individuals in community. We found that within each hub or nodal point of this interdependent web were frictions that did not stagnate progress, but rather kept vital tensions alive. We consider these dynamics as indicative of generative antinomies (Marková, 2003) that keep us questioning meanings-in-contexts. In each of the spatial nodes we have identified thus far, we found evidence of these themes in process.

Our findings indicate that relationship building is a foundational precursor for any change in practice. Additionally, five central processes emerged: building community, being family, communicating, belonging, and becoming (see Figure 2.3 for detail of node). We identified these processes first in the Freedom Market, but realized that within the various initiatives of this community–university team, there were other hubs in which these processes were intentionally and spontaneously co-constructed (see Figure 2.2). We found that transformational pathways situated in the social, cultural, educational, economical, political, and research realms drove and connected these hubs, creating momentum for sustainable change.

For this chapter, we focus on the development of a complex web of interdependent hubs and practices that we call our Interdependence Model. Accessibility to our six central processes across spaces proved essential. We adopted the metaphor of a rhizome (Deleuze & Guattari, 1987) to develop a Model of Interdependence through which we explore how various hubs were connected through these transformational pathways and how redundancy in processes across hubs created new developmental trajectories for community members. This Interdependence Model challenges the notion that learning and change occur in a one-way trajectory or at a single site. Further, it challenges the idea that consensus-based models are adequate for understanding holistic and sustainable change practices. Looking across hubs, we found that transformation processes were generated when multiple and divergent discourses were intentionally allowed to remain in tension, in what we call spaces of dissensus (Ziarek, 2001), rather than being compelled into consensus, which is a direct challenge to the politically correct neatness that has caused well-meaning stakeholders not to address the issues directly. Our findings provide insights into a new and dynamic way of conceptualizing the community as a multi-nodal site for change, where new ways of being manifest in unique but connected ways.

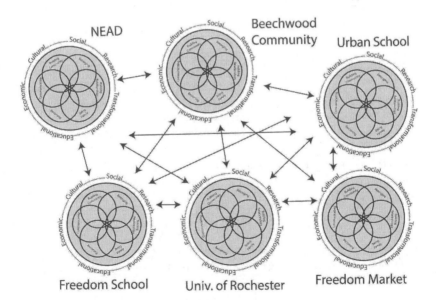

FIGURE 2.2 The Interdependence Model

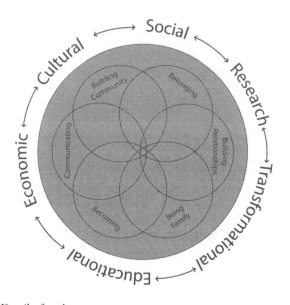

FIGURE 2.3 Detail of node

In the next section, we explain the processes and pathways using examples from our data to illustrate what these processes looked like in everyday interactions, focusing specifically at the Freedom Market site. Figure 2.3 offers a close-up view of one node.

Building Relationships

The first and most foundational process we identified was *building relationships*. Our analysis led us to define building relationships as a process beginning with meeting people "where they are." It required sincerity, compassion, and a willingness to work *with* people as opposed to working *for* people. Relationships were found to develop through what people said and what they did – embodied and communicated directly or indirectly in everyday interactions. Relationships involved a combination of building trust and expecting responsibility—a combination that generated frictions and challenges that were addressed collaboratively. This process proved salient for store personnel, customers, and researchers.

Store personnel at the Market were known collectively as the "Food Corps." The Food Corps was comprised of neighborhood residents hired to work inside the store as "nutrition interventionists." Although they had all the typical duties of store workers, such as stocking shelves and running the cash register, their primary duty was to engage customers and the community in making healthier choices of food consumption by suggesting healthy options for purchase, and even offering recipes and doing food demonstrations. These practices of situated and distributed learning exemplify teaching and learning woven into the everyday interactions of the community. This is not to suggest that there was not push-back from store patrons who were accustomed to established ways of being in this space. Indeed, some community residents (mostly adult males) were resistant to these new interactions at what had been a space in which to "hang out" with (adult male) friends (Field notes, 2/2013). Food Corps workers and the store leadership allowed for this resistance and engaged in respectful dialogue with residents who felt this way. Eventually, this play of difference instituted a new practice between "worthy adversaries" (Mouffe, 1993). Although differences of opinion remained, the differences became a source for almost ritualized joking and banter about a store that had become a research site (Field notes, 2/2013–4/2013). Our analysis of data over time suggests that by allowing the space and time for different ways of being within this space, Market workers allowed for a space of dissensus in which differences did not equate to disrespect—hence relationships could be built despite (in some ways on the basis of) opposing perspectives.

This openness to difference also manifested in forms of assistance to customers whose needs went beyond items in a store. The following interaction was recorded in one researcher's notes:

> Ted is at the front of the store with Wallace (a community elder who works at the store) and Noah (a store employee also from the neighborhood). They have moved away from the activity of the register and are talking in quiet voices with heads down. I can overhear talk about "this time" and Ted seems to be agreeing. They talk over 10 minutes in this way. I find out after Ted leaves that he was trying to borrow money – enough to get him by for a bit.
>
> *(Field notes, 3/2013)*

Rommetveit (1991) notes that shared understanding is an interactional achievement that requires a strong degree of "attunement" to the awareness of the other. At the store, no one taught this; it was not available in a manual or how-to book. Rather, participants learned from each other in processes of relationship building. Building relationships involved trust, but trust was something that was earned. It was negotiated, starting with honest exchanges about everyday life. Instances of tacit "contracts" (Rommetveit, 1991), such as the one involving Ted, in which participants temporarily and partially shared perspectives to make meaning together, appeared in these small ways where mutual respect was subtly (sometimes delicately) offered and tested. Furthermore, university folks had to be real with themselves and acknowledge many of the perceptions and narratives they come in the door with, which could have been construed as "hidden agendas."

Building Community

The second process we identified was *building community*. As the store manager noted, generations ago, barbershops and beauty salons were traditionally the "hubs" in which the broader community related and communicated—establishing informal communities of practice (Lave & Wenger, 1991). With heightened economic disparities in recent years, this sort of consistent, frequent interaction at such community establishments has decreased. Our analyses suggest that Freedom Market, with its model of transformational relationships, has filled this vacancy to become a new community hub. Numerous respondents in interviews and surveys indicated that the store was recognized as a central site for support, reaching across the community. One customer noted that the store is more like a "mom and pop's community store—most of the customers know the staff and they know everyone in here." This perspective reflects the old model of corner stores being owned and operated by folks who lived in the neighborhood, not seen as outsiders. Field notes indicated that it was common for people to stop in several times per day to ask for advice, or seek help with children or elders. One researcher's notes included the following:

> A woman walks in with a folder full of forms—she's having trouble with them. She can't reach anyone for help and isn't sure who to go to. It seems to be some kind of credit assistance program. Wallace asks if I can Google it while they go through the forms together.
>
> *(Field notes, 2/2013)*

The comfort and lack of second-guessing about accessing expertise within the store suggested a developing network of shared expertise, or an informal distributed cognitive system (Hutchins, 1995; Lave & Wenger, 1991). No one was assigned the role of "comforter," "internet information gatherer," etc. Rather, a mutually understood distribution of expertise evolved over time and through interactions across spaces. We found similar instances in which expertise not typically associated with retail business was shared throughout the corpus of field data, including the following:

- A teenager called from school when he was being sent home so that someone could notify his mom.
- A six-year-old came by to share his report card with the adults at the store.
- A mother called the store to ask Wallace to speak to her teenaged daughter, whom the mother fears is getting involved with a dangerous crowd.

(Field notes, 3/2012–4/2013)

This sense of a new kind of community, emerging spontaneously but with intentionality, was observed to be evolving within the store as both workers and community members came to recognize and value the distributed expertise of Food Corps workers, management, customers, and even university researchers.

Being Family

The third process we identified was *being family*. A regular customer described the Market this way: "this is my family from another mother." It was also called a "safe haven, my home away from home." This notion of a new, homelike space was observed as children and adults visited the store up to ten times per day, taking items from the store's coolers as one would a refrigerator in their own home. We began to uncover how the community came to see and co-construct the store as a "homeplace" (hooks, 1990). Robert, the store manager, noted "people have come to trust us with their lives." He recounted how one day:

> A woman who was about to faint due to her diabetes came into the store. She just sat on the stoop, and then proceeded to lie down. She told him she had been diagnosed two days earlier with diabetes. Robert notes, "having recently been diagnosed with diabetes myself, I knew to give her orange juice." When she was able to stand, she expressed how thankful she was for the first aid provided.
>
> *(Field notes, 2/2013)*

Our data suggested that the Market became a safe haven, a place for nurturing in times of need, and a space in which family-like experiences, such as doing homework and chatting about medical concerns, were everyday occurrences. hooks's (1990) notion of "homeplace" is helpful for understanding this dynamic as not only comforting, but also powerfully and politically transformative. That is, "homeplace" complicates assumptions about marginality or outsidedness by pointing out the powerful covert capacities for resistance within spaces from the "margins," as margins are the very ideal spaces for "others" to "meet." hooks makes the case that these spheres of cultural practice and sites of resistance have always been there, operating under the radar without recognition or validation from a dominant vantage point. Seen in this light, the store as a site that fosters new ways of being family is a politically and socially potent site for change. This is contrary to the local trend that sees corner stores as places of loitering and illegal behavior, which caused the City of Rochester in 2013 to establish new, more restrictive zoning for corner stores to address neighborhood complaints.

Communicating

The fourth process we identified was *communicating*. Communicating builds on the idea of the store as a hub, a resource and a gathering space. Data indicated that the store was seen as a place to get information and to share stories and cultural values, particularly regarding what was going on in the neighborhood. This was found to occur in at least two ways: spontaneously and intentionally.

Sometimes communicative practices at the store seemed primarily spontaneous and organic. For example, on one occasion, a customer stopped in and asked when a community member's wake was scheduled. On another occasion, a customer asked about applications for local housing. Here, there were no constraints on what counted as a "valid" topic of conversation. Rather, dialogicality was emergent and situation-specific: conversations evolved organically, and they were often personal, sometimes "gossipy," and very often highly political. One researcher noted the following:

> When Wallace came in I asked him, "Why were you carrying those newspaper articles in your pocket that day?" He said that he often carries articles with him. He said that, at first, he keeps articles for his own information. He shared that, eventually, he uses the articles to initiate conversations with community members and to challenge what is going on. He referred again to the fact that the city school district is the last in the country for Black and Latino males. "It makes you question what's going on," he added. Wallace concluded that it is important for him to encourage his community to take a more active role in the education of its youth because "it takes a village."
>
> (Field notes, 3/2013)

Wallace's comment points to the other way that communications were seen to occur at the store—as the result of intentionality, a part of the new space/way of being that is being constructed. Another example of this was identified in the way that Food Corps workers distributed Family Nutrition Records to community members. The official purpose of these forms was to track the amount of fruit, vegetables, and sugary drinks families consumed on a weekly basis. The numerical data was being gathered for funders. At the same time, however, Food Corps workers used these forms to initiate dialogues about eating habits and food purchasing practices in the interest of fostering positive measurable results. Through everyday interactions such as these, Market staff would consistently "check in" with customers. As a result, they knew what was going on with families in the neighborhood.

Whether intentional or spontaneous, communicating in this space was dialogic and synergistic (Bakhtin, 1981; community member, 2012). It was observable as a practice-in-development, filled with tensions, the easing of tension, and the generation of new tensions (Marková, 2003). Engaged participants worked through these frictions as respectful participants in authentic dialogue. To responsibly consider learning, conversation, mediation, and change practices within the store and among the research team, we needed to recognize the varied histories of the individuals, the community, and the broader sociopolitical sphere that impacted store interactions. We found that concepts from radical democracy, which see difference and struggle as generative, productive, and necessary for ethical political engagement (Laclau & Mouffe, 1985; Mouffe, 1993), were far more effective for understanding the practices our research examined than were political models that foreground normative consistency or consensus building.

Belonging

The fifth process we identified was *belonging*. People who came to the store noted feeling acknowledged for who they were, in a non-judgmental way. A customer told a research team member, "Before, they didn't do that. ... But the store here, I feel you come in here and it doesn't matter who you are, people are always kind and curious and respectful to you." As noted above, even individuals with irreconcilable points of view seemed to find ways to be authentic—knowing their views were respected, even if not condoned—in this community space.

Some participants noted that churches and schools no longer seemed necessarily to offer sites for belonging, but that as a community hub, the Market was emerging as one place where they felt this sense of belonging. Further, many acknowledged that this sense of belonging was new to them. In one team meeting, a researcher identified this feeling in himself:

> They came, they're like they'll just, I want to do something. I like how this makes me feel. I feel at home, some it's like church ... so they want to contribute. So they say how can I contribute to the way I feel. I feel good and I'm matching this feeling. I belong. I want to help.
> *(Team meeting transcript, 9/2013)*

The researcher's reflection on his own learning pathway was telling. It suggested that he was not only observing, but also starting to feel like a part of the community and processes being observed. The boundaries between roles and places were in flux or tension, but the desire to belong and to be part of the change processes came through. This sense of nascent processes is a key factor in our sixth process: becoming.

Becoming

The last process we identified was *becoming*. Becoming implies the sense of change going on in the store and in the community (what we have identified as a shift from the transactional to the transformational). We found that this process was taking place at multiple levels—within individuals, among customers at the store, among the community members who work in and run the store, and among university research partners who found our roles evolving in unexpected ways.

An employee of a local community development organization who started working in the store explained:

> I found myself at the store more and more. I no longer wanted to just come to the store, I wanted to be part of the store. As I visited more, I found what was supposed to work for our community members was working on me as well. My role transitioned from being served to now serving. So how does one go from being the educator to being educated? No longer do I have an extended hand, but now a connected one.
> (Memo, 3/2013)

As community members themselves, the community activists who purchased the store and the Food Corps members placed high value on the human capital of this community, and held high expectations for the community's capacity to come to know and understand what needed to be done for lasting, substantive change. For them, the store was a restorative space that could help the community "get itself back in order" (because perceptions from insiders and outsiders suggested that it had been out of order for too long). Although they drew from local traditions to enact these processes of change, store leaders made this space intentionally creative and new. They explored opportunities for fresh ways of keeping people engaged through creative expression and ways of combining marketability with ethics—being very "cutting edge" and yet very "old school" (Field notes, 9/2012; 2/2013). Store staff were observed to consistently engage the community in creative ways to celebrate successes, and in ways to mediate problems through restorative justice practices so that consequences were fairly meted out for failures to be responsible to the newly developing, shared expectations of the emerging vision, or for contradicting the central values that were being solidified.

This double sentiment, of both old school practical wisdom and almost metaphysical attention to care of the other, might seem at first to be contradictory. Our analysis indicates, however, that such simultaneity of difference is a regular component of the agonistic, dialogical practices that took place here, and were part of what fueled its transformational capabilities and hence cleared new pathways.

Interdependent Nodes and Transformational Pathways

Within and across hubs, we identified transformational pathways. We found that the store was a social space; that it built on cultural practices of food as well as practices of restorative justice ("good food for good people"); that it created economies through opportunities for the dollars earned in the community to stay in the community; that politics and policies framed the everyday business of the store and many of the conversations, from school policies to drug laws; that it was an educational space where homework was done, forms were completed, and job training took place; and that it was a research site (as noted on the flyer posted on the door and on the side of the cooler) where community practices and processes of transformation were documented. We argue that nurturing and making these pathways explicit enervates the hubs by creating momentum toward change. One researcher observed at a meeting:

> I just want to point out that it's not just spontaneously transformational, right, it's intentional. Because initially coming in they were standoffish, back, but now they come in with their problems, whether it's cultural, social, economics ... coming to understand the value of being within your neighborhood.
> *(Team meeting transcript, 2013)*

The transformational pathways we identified were not static, but rather dynamically interconnected to, and affected by, the different hubs within the whole rhizomatic network.

We came to our conceptual frameworks as a result of ongoing and collaborative attempts to make sense of our data. We often found ourselves struggling to find terms for the complexities and overlapping processes and ways of meaning making we were seeing. Dialogicality served to make sense of how meaning was constructed between and among persons, spaces, and times. We found that Deleuze and Guattari's (1987) concept of the rhizome helped to make sense of the ways in which the store, local schools, and other organizations (see Figure 2.2) appeared to be distinct and separate, but actually had complex subterranean connections. The rhizome gave us a metaphor with which to explain how new ideas "took off" in new and unexpected directions, developing into new hubs or nodes that functioned alone, but remained connected to the store and the community. We propose that these "hubs of interdependence" stand in contrast to the ideologies of independence that drive many policies, social structures, and notions of family in the United States. For example, we found that economies in the store were connected with the community development organization across the street and the lives of community members. Likewise, the cultural framework of the Freedom School, with the foundation of the nine principles of *nguzo saba* (discussed in Chapter 4), was present in the store through service, unity, and community. Further, community members and parents at the school have become co-researchers along with university faculty and students, who use community-defined evidence to inform practices, to present together at conferences, and to write grant applications.

Conclusion

We have discussed how we constructed our Interdependence Model and given examples of the processes and pathways we identified. Our research began at the Freedom Market (see Chapter 5), but crossed into new spaces, as six common processes were nurtured across other hubs in the community. Our data demonstrate how, in each space, these processes were intentionally and spontaneously co-constructed by community members and university researchers. Furthermore, we suggest that movement across these hubs creates "transformational pathways" toward a larger activist network. We found that these "travels" constituted new developmental trajectories through which community members constructed new and changing ways of being, in community, and suggest that by making these practices explicit, other community researchers can develop transformational pathways relevant to the communities they serve.

We close with our latest endeavor to build connections among the various nodes in our work and to enact the *kuumba* (creativity) principle of *nguzo saba* by making the space more beautiful than we found it. Our community mural projects[2] emerged as we imagined together that the walls on Freedom Market and the NEAD main office across the street could have murals to represent who we are. The research team conceived of the murals as standing for the interaction of word and image. The first mural (left-hand photo in Figure 2.4) is rooted in the mission of *nguzo saba* with the explicit placing of words on stones along the path to freedom. The mission in the second mural (right-hand photo in Figure 2.4) would be seen through the sankofa bird, which symbolizes reaching back into history to frame the future. What emerged was a set of murals that would be connected through visual messages and intentionally placed locations to represent cultural history, activism, and commitments to the principles of *nguzo saba* that are deeply rooted in African American culture in this neighborhood.

The murals have become spaces for dialogic constructions of pathways to transformation for individuals and for the community as a whole. People

FIGURE 2.4 Community mural projects.[3] Photographs by Joanne Larson (left) and Shane Wiegand (right)

gather to look in silence or to talk about what they mean. "Where does the road to freedom lead?" provides an entry point into speaking across difference and into building relationships. Potential for transformation lies in those relationships and how those relationships lead to building community and to sustaining that community.

The next chapter goes more deeply into how the research team realized we were experiencing the same transformations that were occurring in the other hubs.

Notes

1 Ideas in this chapter have been presented at two research conferences: Larson, J., Hanny, C., Duckles, J., Moses, G., Wu, X., Moses, R., Brown, K., Smith, W., & Smith, J. (2013, April) *Community literacies as shared resources for transformation*, paper presented at the annual meeting of the American Educational Research Association, San Francisco, CA and Larson, J., Duckles, J., Hanny, C., Gallegos Greenwich, J., & Moses, G. (2014, June) *"It's intentional": Co-construction of transformational processes and pathways within and across hubs of interdependence in an urban community*, paper presented at the International Conference of Learning Sciences, Boulder, CO.
2 Portions of this section appear in Larson, J., Hanny, C., Duckles, J., Pham, H., Moses, R., & Moses, G. (2017). Expressing community through Freedom Market and visual connections in *The Art and Craft of Literacy Pedagogy: Profiling Community Arts Zone*. Special Issue of *Pedagogies: An International Journal*, 12:1, 4–20, DOI:10.1080/1554480X.2017.1283999.
3 This work was partially supported by the Social Sciences and Humanities Research Council of Canada (grant number 430-2013-1025).

References

Bakhtin, M. (1981). *The dialogic imagination*. M. Holquist (Ed.), M. Holquist & C. Emerson (Trans.). Austin, TX: University of Texas Press.

Deleuze, G. & Guattari, F. (1987). *A thousand plateaus: Capitalism and schizophrenia*. Minneapolis, MN: University of Minnesota Press.

Emdin, C. (2013). *Pedagogies for social change*. Keynote speech delivered at Hip-Hop Literacies Conference, The Ohio State University, Columbus, OH.

hooks, b. (1990). *Yearning*. New York, NY: South End.

Hutchins, E. (1995). *Cognition in the wild*. Cambridge, MA: The MIT Press.

Laclau, E. & Mouffe, C. (1985). *Hegemony as socialist strategy: Toward a radical democratic politics*. London, UK: Verso.

Larson, J., Duckles, J., Hanny, C., Gallegos Greenwich, J., & Moses, G. (2014, June). *"It's intentional": Co-construction of transformational processes and pathways within and across hubs of interdependence in an urban community*. Paper presented at the International Conference of Learning Sciences, Boulder, CO.

Larson, J., Hanny, C., Duckles, J., Moses, G., Wu, X., Moses, R., Brown, K., Smith, W., & Smith, J. (2013, April). *Community literacies as shared resources for transformation*. Paper presented at the annual meeting of the American Educational Research Association, San Francisco, CA.

Larson, J., Hanny, C., Duckles, J., Pham, H., Moses, R., & Moses, G. (2017). "Expressing community through Freedom Market and visual connections" in *The Art and Craft of Literacy Pedagogy: Profiling Community Arts Zone*. Special Issue of *Pedagogies: An International Journal, 12*(1), 4–20, DOI:10.1080/1554480X.2017.1283999.

Lave, J. & Wenger, E. (1991). *Situated learning: Legitimate peripheral participation*. Cambridge, UK: University of Cambridge Press.

Leander, K. & Boldt, G. (2013). Rereading "A pedagogy of multiliteracies": Bodies, texts, and emergence. *Journal of Literacy Research, 45*(1), 22–46.

Leander, K. & Rowe, D. (2006). Mapping literacy spaces in motion: A rhizomatic analysis of a classroom literacy performance. *Reading Research Quarterly, 41*(4), 428–460.

Marková, I (2003). *Dialogicality and social representations: The dynamics of mind*. Cambridge, UK: Cambridge University Press.

Mouffe, C. (1993). *Return of the political*. London, UK: Verso.

Rommetveit, R. (1991). On axiomatic features of a dialogic approach to language and mind. In I. Marková & K. Foppa, (Eds.) *The dynamics of dialogue*. New York, NY: Springer-Verlag.

Ziarek, E.P. (2001). *An ethics of dissensus: Postmodernity, feminism, and the politics of radical democracy*. Stanford, CA: Stanford University Press.

3

WHEN THEORY MET PRACTICE

Methodology in the Versus

Courtney Hanny, Joyce Duckles, Jeremy Smith, Robert Moses, Joel Gallegos Greenwich

>*Versus*: 1400–50, late Middle English < Latin: towards, i.e., turned so as to face (something), opposite, over against, orig. past participle of *vertere* to turn
>
>*Conversation*: mid-14th century, "living together, having dealings with others," also "manner of conducting oneself in the world"; from Old French *conversation*, from Latin *conversationem* (nominative *conversatio*) "act of living with," noun of action from past participle stem of *conversari* "to live with, keep company with," literally "turn about with" ...
>
> (Online Etymology Dictionary)

Getting to a Point

"You know," Robert said, leaning forward and pointing his finger, "you know a lot about *us*, but we don't know about *you*." And then, something occurred that was very rare among this research team: silence. "You come in and ask all kinds of questions, but nobody asks questions of you. It only goes in one direction." It's likely this silence had multiple sources. For community members, the direct challenge reflected something a lot of us had been thinking but hadn't said. For the university members, the direct challenge struck at the heart of what we stood for as activist, justice-minded researchers—after all, we were all about reciprocity. Weren't we? Could it be that we had been blind to this unidirectionality? Seemed so.

This uncomfortable moment of truth was an important turning point in the story of our team's evolution—and an example of what we have come to recognize as an effect of generative frictions that foster news ways of researching and constructing knowledge together. In this case, the challenge of unidirectionality caused us to rethink, collectively, how we understood (or failed to understand) participatory research. It wasn't enough simply to be physically present observing, or to "share" our skills, or "teach" our methods. Such assumptions, in fact, can mask epistemological inequities—valuing some forms of knowledge and failing to recognize others. That is, even the most progressive and justice-minded approaches to social and educational research frequently maintain tacit assumptions that the "knowledge" produced by the research will be filtered through and validated by extant paradigms as determined by academic institutions. The presumption that we, as university researchers, were to teach community researchers how to do research and how to recognize what counts as evidence was a false premise, grounded upon an unjustifiable epistemological hierarchy. It is worth noting that as we collectively reconstructed the vignette above, George noted that Robert's question had indeed been posed before, by various community researchers, but it had not been answered. Which is to say, up until the point of Robert's direct challenge, we had somehow not registered similar previous comments as protests or challenges to our assumptions about how to do research. So how did we get to Robert's point? And where did we go from there? At least two "turns" toward increasing recognition of the importance of relationships foreshadowed Robert's point.

Relational Turns

Not long into our initial research process, we realized we needed to step back from our focus on grocery shopping and food practices, and pay closer attention to the complexities and nuances of trust and relationship building between store workers and patrons. Let's face it—nobody from the community was sharing anything without that. Who would be allowed into homes to request these stories? Why would patrons share personal stories with new owners whose intentions in taking over the store might not be entirely clear? Why should patrons seek or accept advice from new store workers? We were starting to sense a dialogical learning space developing within the store, but how was that happening? What conditions make it so that someone will share their story—or be open to letting you share yours? And what did these possibilities mean for university researchers—decidedly outsiders? We had to slow our speed and shift our gaze. And it worked. Trust happened, but it was for invested community partners—not outside researchers—to determine the pace.

Months before Robert's more direct challenge to the group, he had initiated a similar turn regarding research practices at the store. Early in the project, when university researchers documented interactions in the Market, they used traditional methods of observing and note taking. We would sit by the door, or at the counter, interacting with customers and helping fill out surveys on the computer, and take copious field notes to be shared later with the team. But Robert pushed us to rethink that paradigm—to do store work, to take on roles other than "researcher" (a role not recognized as valuable to the community patrons in the Market). He knew this was the way to build relationships, and it was genuinely "economic" (a matter of reciprocity and exchange in which values were mutually understood) as well. In the new paradigm, everyone in the store—researcher or community worker—*worked the store*. With newbie university folks at the cash register, when the unexpected happened (like the price scanner failing with a line of customers), patient customers joked and poked fun as they eased the nervous cashier's growing panic, talking them through pricing items and entering them manually. This change ushered in a different way of understanding expertise and the sharing of knowledge—community members were teaching researchers how to *be*, authentically, in the store and community. They talked us through entering numbers in boxes and rows at the lottery machine. In turn, customers became accustomed to us writing field notes and other researcher practices. Occasionally, a regular customer would make sure a researcher noticed something going on in the store: "D'gya get that? Make sure you write that down!" They jokingly scolded researchers if we missed our typical day at the store: "Where do you think you were yesterday!?!"

These events illustrate the progression, over time and through various iterations, of our movement toward increasingly relational practices, implicating greater personal vulnerability, intimacy, and trust. Joyce has made the point throughout the research team's evolution that the team has come to function like a family: internally, we're going to be hard on each other, and challenge each other and disagree, but in the long run, we have each other's backs. This sort of familiar architecture is not a matter of signing a contract or agreeing to a code of conduct. It is ongoing work of building and rebuilding relationships, and sticking with it. Why does it matter—this turn toward the personal and relational? We suggest that the (micro) interactions of researching together reflect the challenges and potentialities of (macro) paradigms regarding social structures, symbolic capital and whose knowledge counts (epistemological justice).

In this chapter, we tell the stories of the evolution of the research team as a working body, the ongoing adaptations of our methodologies and practices, and the development of our co-constructed, guiding concepts, as they were developed within, and reflect, generative frictions, dissensus, and a distributed, rhizomatic approach to knowledge production. Most of these stories depict conversations—talk that genuinely reflects the etymological roots of the term: the act of "turning" + "with." We give specific attention to how we interpret, critique, and deploy a version of participatory action research, and community literacy practices and products that reflect and encourage dialogicality and epistemic equality (Fricker, 2007; Postma, 2016). We contend that the collection of stories in this chapter serves as an intervention on three fronts. First, it works to challenge the power disparities that characterize many university/community partnerships. Second, it contributes to a complex understanding of literacy practices as socially constructed, culturally relevant, and locally defined. And third, the stories contribute to a powerful emerging force in research paradigms that challenge epistemic injustice by prioritizing authentic unique approaches to participatory methods and activism.

Epistemological Justice and Community/University Partnerships

The last ten years have seen a sharp increase in efforts on the part of universities to partner or otherwise become more involved with/in their local communities. Whether in the form of community service, engaged learning, or—as in our particular case—participatory research—there is growing recognition that universities need to bolster local communities, rather than merely existing as isolated, elite silos—cut off from the realities of life outside the campus borders. But the problem is that such efforts are often cosmetic, leaving unexamined assumptions about what counts as knowledge and who defines it—hence doing what Fricker (2007) refers to as epistemic injustice, or what Larson (in Kinloch, Larson, Faulstich Orellana, & Lewis, 2016) refers to as, a "neoliberal rescue fantasy" (p. 65) and producing nothing of measurable "use" to community members (Gutiérrez & Penuel, 2014). In the preface to their book on engaged scholarship, Shultz and Kajner (2013) encourage researchers to ask, whose knowledge counts? How is knowledge constructed and/or co-constructed? How do we support knowledge strategies that build capacity for movements for change? How do we support our own personal processes of de-colonization as well as de-colonization of higher education itself? At universities where funding is often a primary concern for administrations, there may be less desire to experiment with emergent and novel approaches to research that don't have established precedent in research literature and no guarantee of financial pay off by way of grants from the most prestigious funding institutions—these projects can be a tough "sell" if measured solely by quantifiable criteria determined by academic institutions. Further, despite the doubtlessly good intentions to respond to calls for engaged scholarship and community partnerships, institutions may fail to be adequately prepared for the complexities of these projects (Curwood et al., 2011). The Freedom Market collaboration, from the beginning, intended to defy these precedents.

It was noted in Chapter 1 that George, knowing that he wanted the Market project to be more than just a business venture, but also a documented and powerful contribution to social change discourses, drew upon his longstanding relationship with Joanne. Past experiences and lessons learned led George to believe that, although he and his colleagues knew how to do community change—and do it *right*—they, like many neighborhood organizations across the country, didn't make a habit of documenting and recording the processes as data—they just did the work. That's where the university could come in, giving some "textual" expertise to document the "action" expertise at which NEAD excelled. In the early months of the project, we thought we would be studying cooking practices in neighborhood homes and food shopping practices at the store. After a few preliminary sessions talking about the basics of interviewing techniques, how to gain consents, and the subtleties of taking qualitative field notes, the research began. It was only in retrospect that we recognized that, despite our own good intentions, we still maintained three presumptions regarding our process/methods: first, we thought the process would consist of university researchers showing community members "how to" do research; second, we thought the primary subjects of inquiry would be residents and food practices; and third, we thought that reflexivity was something that could be managed and scheduled. That is, we thought that methodology would determine practices. The reality turned out to be far more circuitous and unpredictable.

Usually working in teams of two or three, with both university and community members, we conducted site observations and in-home interviews, inquiring about what community members were eating; how meals were organized and prepared in households; and how such practices had changed over generations, reflecting changes in community/family life over time. What sorts of meanings and significances were associated with the histories of food practices in the neighborhood? What could a vision of the future borrow from memories of the past? If some aspects of community or family had been lost through recent decades, how might they be recouped? The way in was food, but we were clearly asking for more complex histories, memories, and testimonials—stories to help us better "make sense" of things—how were these practices part of a complex way of life? What did these interactions and traditions mean to people who lived, worked, and raised families in this neighborhood? We were hungry to gather up all the stories and histories available—eager to understand the complex, big picture.

But we had to begin seeing one another as equal but different holders of knowledge, establishing roles of novice and expert according to context, and flexible enough to drop those roles and take on others as time, situations, and contexts evolved. In short, we found ourselves needing to practice the sort of radical democratic approach discussed in Chapter 2, in which contextual and historical power disparities were recognized and respected, rather than hidden or neutralized. Generative frictions in conversation led to the political and epistemological ideas of dissensus/pluralist agonism and dialogicality, respectively. As Dempsey (2010) put it,

> Campus–community partnerships are characterized by inequalities of power that impede collaboration and introduce conflicts. Despite these inherent tensions, much of the literature implies that community is easily located and defined and that community representation is nonproblematic.
>
> (p. 360)

For us, addressing the complexities and nuances of authentically engaged, dialogic, democratic work that would meet the criteria of local use meant making changes and reflecting critically on our ways of working. Our group coding sessions show how our practices evolved.

From Coding to Conversing to Co-authoring: Letting Go of Predetermined Methods

Our first session of coding together started as a quiet and orderly process, with flip charts, etc., as the university researchers understood the steps of grounded theory and participatory action research (PAR) (see Figure 2.1 in Chapter 2). And we *did* develop a list of categories and emergent themes. But our most salient findings at the early stages came when our conversations moved away from a linear progression and shifted to a more rhizomatic practice—and got deeply into meanings of terms and concepts—these were often tied to very personal, strongly held ideas that connoted different histories and not-necessarily-compatible perspectives. For example, when we began to collaboratively develop our notion of "rhizome" (see Chapter 2), everyone took out their phones to look up what this meant, to share pictures, and make connections to the concept. One community member said, "we call that grassroots." This congruence of understanding resulted in the adoption of the rhizome as a guiding theme in our work. The term reflects a shared understanding of the underground connections that we all wanted to make intentional.

In the beginning, we held an assumption that collaboration would mean that we would work together to collect and analyze data, and that the university researchers would show the store workers and community researchers the ways that PAR and ethnographic research was done (for example, how to take field notes, do open coding, and analyze data). But we came to see that our collaborations *were* data, being generated through our interactions. We needed to attend to our understandings (or misunderstandings) of what our work and our relationships meant. The process, therefore, was more personal, complex, and less tidy than a protocol could contain. "Generative frictions," served not only as a conceptual metaphor for the data on the store and the neighborhood, but also as a reflection of the research team's evolution.

In this way, collectively making sense of the work and of these dynamics has been a central topic at research team meetings, which we started holding weekly about a year into the project. At these meetings, we typically start with a tentative agenda, but we discuss any pressing issues that arise, as they arise. It has happened that an unexpected topic or a point that seemed like a small detail engenders a full meeting's worth of attention. It was such an unplanned collective session that gave rise to our rhizomatic Model of Interdependence, as detailed in the previous chapters.

This was one example of how two discourse communities came together and adopted each other's terms. This story set the stage for various frictions that fueled the generativity and creativity of our work. The initial tensions between the scholarly approach of the university and the lived-experience approach of the community researchers surfaced more vividly than the university researchers expected, as reflected in the story that opens this chapter. Even though the university researchers took pride in understanding engagement and activist research, frictions (generative or not) between an academic approach and a life-experience approach demanded that we turn our gaze to these differences and what they meant.

Part of challenging what counts as research is reconsidering what counts as evidence. The best-intentioned researchers often fail at participatory interventions because they fail to do what Flower (2008) might refer to as their "rhetorical homework" (p. 88). That is, they fail to find out what community members think and feel about policies, programs—and, importantly, university interventions—often rooted in complicated histories that are not immediately visible. Avoiding such a failure requires at least two significant responsibilities to be accepted by university researchers. First, it requires responsibility to the cultural history of the community's interactions with universities and other institutions. Negative past experiences can have long-lasting effects of distrust or hostility. The second responsibility is related to the first, and consists in taking *time*. Distrust and/or hostilities are often deep-rooted, and it is unlikely that they will be brought up right away. Handing out a survey or conducting a single interview or focus group is unlikely to elicit the kind of meaningful testimony that can help improve understanding. If there is one mantra our team has adopted across the board, it is that *building relationships* is absolutely necessary as a precursor, as well as an ongoing process, for collecting data and encouraging dialogue and for accomplishing and sustaining the kind of transformational change we are working toward. Genuine conversation, with all its attendant dialogicality, agonism, and unpredictability, *is* method.

Conversations Turning on Frictions: Developing Theory in the Versus

It seems so obvious now, but it took us a while to realize that the exact same questions applied to us. That is, the processes we were observing at the store were occurring with us, as a team—these same tensions about trust existed within our small group. We had a lot of work to do to build up mutual trust and to work through complicated divergences in perspectives and ways of thinking/speaking ("competing discourses" as we have come to call them). We *knew* we all had different strengths and areas of expertise, but that's not the same thing as *understanding* how they work together. It was, after all, almost a year into the process before the afternoon when Robert challenged the university researchers to be vulnerable to bidirectional research (*When do we learn about you?*). In other words, our acknowledgement of difference in discourses and expertise could not presume a shared perspective or understanding—these had to be negotiated and worked through. How did we address this?

After Robert posed his challenge about the unidirectionality of the research, it was decided that we needed to take a break from the routine of weekly meetings at the NEAD office and get to know each other on a more social level. We began the practice of breaking bread together—both literally (at an inaugural dinner at Joanne's house, followed by similar events at the Freedom School cafe and the homes of other research team members) and figuratively (see hooks and West's (1999) *Breaking Bread*, on the connections between authentic community building in culturally, racially, and historically relevant scholarship).

Joanne's offer to open her home to the group for our first breaking bread represented a significant act of trust. Unknown to everyone on the research team but George, Joanne and her husband Morris had not had guests in their home for over ten years. Their youngest son Marcus has Tourette Syndrome, OCD, and ADHD and has serious behavioral issues, oftentimes quite violent. Because of this, they did not have people over. When Robert challenged the university members of the team to open their spaces to community members, Joanne went all in and invited them over. It proved to be a significant moment for her family and deepened her trust in the team.

After this inaugural dinner, the team went to Kim's for a housewarming. This was followed by a holiday dinner at Joyce's that has now become tradition. George and other community members have come to the university to give presentations and many of them have presented at national and international research conferences about our work. Recently, Joyce has presented with community members on the team at community development conferences and gone with George to meetings at the Mayor's office. Joanne and Joyce served on the Board of Education Committee with community members. Community members went through Institutional Review Board (IRB) training and have moved to formal investigative roles on research projects. We now find ourselves in each others' spaces and places on a regular basis.

We had some tough discussions about topics on which we had (and often still have) differing perspectives, as the stories in this chapter and the following chapters illustrate. We reflected upon the meanings of these interactions themselves, initiating a habit of reflection, reflexivity, and writing together. These three practices are interdependent, but nothing happens without the first two. Coming back to the model, questioning what is working and making necessary changes keeps things new—keeps us from falling into a stagnant monologicality (a risk when you take the relationships or the model for granted). In short, we see dissensus, rhizomatic knowledge production, and generative frictions more as practices than as simply abstract concepts.

Dissensus, Rhizomes, and Generative Frictions as Practices

"Dissensus" gave us a way of talking about and wrapping our heads around our extant, sometimes frustrating, but also idea-inspiring, frictions. We found various points of convergence and divergence around different issues. In some cases, some, we let the issues lie in contradiction—we didn't need to resolve them or come to agreement. Rather, we found that when we let differences guide our conversations, new, often creative and unforeseen, ideas emerged. Co-conceptualizing what we were seeing and doing in the store, and across other hubs, and as a team became the act of grappling with unpredictability to forge something new. In doing so, we were able to resist tendencies to fall into scripted narratives about how to behave in engagements with others, to rely on fixed normative criteria, or to essentialize, stereotype, or presume fixity regarding group identities, and instead develop counterstories, and encourage counterpublics (Flower, 2008). Rather than knowledge being transmitted linearly from person(s) to person(s), knowledge was generated and challenged and developed in the intersubjective, overlapping, often messy spaces between persons. Below we share stories around two, related frictions that have proven generative for fostering new ways of being, working, and making meaning together. It should be noted that when we use the term "versus," we are invoking its rich etymological meaning, not a binary or polarity between two opposed parties (it should be clear by now that we eschew any such linear interpretations). Rather, we see the versus as those points of turning together and against that reflect and perpetuate generative frictions in a space of dissensus.

Friction 1: Feminism Versus Fatherhood

In the first few months of our presence in the newly opened Market, several university researchers had made similar observations, suggesting that the store felt like a masculine space. We had not yet established our practice of meeting regularly as a group, but the university researchers met on campus between classes, so this common thread came up in conversation. Many of the university researchers on the project identified as feminist, and gendered social interactions were things we were accustomed to noticing and to discussing. Joanne addressed this observation in a private discussion with George, thinking that she could help him to better understand gender dynamics at the store, as if the community team members hadn't thought through the implications of the store as a masculine space.

Two things occurred, stretched across a few months. First, George shifted the conversation with Joanne to invoke what he referred to as the Father Legacy. In fact, he brought Robert in, by phone, to help him explain. As Robert told Joanne on the phone, the store was deliberately constructed to be a recuperative space to restore a community in which adult men (especially Black men) were often, for various sociohistorical reasons, absent from community or family life. The values promoted by the new, transformative store, were intended to restore the stability of the patriarchal presence—including respecting women and very intentionally working against objectifying women.

The Father Legacy provided an essential layer to understanding dynamics at the store. But the conversation didn't end there. George and Robert were offended that it had been implied they had been chauvinistic or allowed for chauvinism at the store. In response, George consulted with other community members to get their perceptions on the question and called for another meeting with Joanne, Joyce, and Courtney. While the university women worked hard to make the case that feminism was not about challenging men but equality for all, George worked hard to make the case that whereas the store had indeed been a male/patriarchal space in the past, the new space was radically family-oriented. It was a highly generative meeting—much was learned about each person's perspective. But this was one of the occasions that led the group to realize we needed to meet as a whole team, and meet frequently, to clear the air or gain clarity on others' perceptions and interpretations. And this is what we mean by a generative friction—the concepts of feminism versus fatherhood remain contested, but it is the processes of working through and around the differences that gives rise to the new and unexpected. Almost two years after the initial question about masculine spaces, the team was discussing what it meant to "stand" with the community (see Chapter 5 for the story). As happened on several occasions, the discussion tapped into the feminism versus fatherhood question. And at one point, George did something unexpected. First, he asked if the whole group was willing to get real with the conversation, checking with each person individually. Each of us agreed, and we all agreed to turn off the camera and audio recorder. Then, each person responded, in their own way, to the prompt, "Tell me about your father."

The result was a powerful, emotional, and long conversation that was far from what anyone expected that day, but that strengthened the group's trust in one another and deepened our capacities to recognize the complex, historical, and personal histories that came to bear on our collective, shared, or disputed ways of making sense of our data and the world, and how our past experiences shape our present perceptions.

Why was it important to leave the concept "in friction"? We argue that there is much more to gain by continuing the dialogue without diluting the potency of either stance than there is in coming to a watered-down consensus that does not adequately represent what anyone truly thinks or feels. This is what we mean by dissensus. It is in some ways adversarial, but it includes the recognition of others as worthy, respected adversaries. Additionally, when the frictions are allowed to remain in play, albeit more often than not in the background (we aren't always attending to every difference, of course), we continue to learn. Which is to say, differences will arise in new contexts, adding new layers of meaning and complexity to issues as they arise. For example, another generative friction that informed our interactions, which we see as differing approaches to activism, is enriched by understanding the feminism/fatherhood friction.

Friction 2: Approaches to Activism: FIGHT Versus Relational Activism

The second generative friction is related, but this one is less a direct topic of conversation than a difference of perspectives that informed our interactions, and it regards approaches to social justice and activism. As discussed in Chapter 1, Rochester has a long history as a site for social and racial justice, including FIGHT, in which Wallace was an important figure. FIGHT, or *Freedom Independence God Honor Today*, Rochester's affiliate of the Black Power movement, made self-determination, spirituality, and solidarity its central tenets. "I'm not radical; I'm determined," informed the group's collective actions. As such, FIGHT rejected a strict adherence to nonviolence in the face of violence. Not to fight back would equate to allowing oneself and one's history to be named and determined by an (oppressive, colonizing) other—it would be to deny *kujichagulia*, self-determination, one of the *nguzo saba* tenets. FIGHT's legacy of activism lives in various nodes of the Freedom Market project. George's description of current practices at the Freedom School men's meetings reflect these historical roots:

> When you're coming to a group of men at Freedom School it's very intentional. We believe in the living God, we pray every morning. From the experience of Black men ... you know black men did not have a name. The men here know that history, we thought that by coming here, you would come to understand the history. We study American history to see how we fit into it. So if you've only understood American history, you're going to miss a whole part of it.
>
> *(Writing team meeting, 2/2017)*

In these ways, the traditions of more identity-based, militant, or resistance oriented activism differ from the approaches that foreground dialogue and relationship building (the university researchers' primary approach), although the desired ends to both are the eradication of inequality in all its overt and covert guises. At team meetings, the differences in approach revealed themselves mostly in terms of the metaphors we employed. For example, George and

Robert often invoked battle metaphors to describe the work they were doing to transform the community. Joel and Joanne often refer to Freire's (1998) notion of radical love and lessons from the local Gandhi Institute make their way into our discourses. Although these approaches clash in some discussions, they can also be seen as generating work on multiple fronts (i.e., through the various hubs and nodes that make up the Interdependence Model) and function differently in terms of symbolic, material, embodied, and relational modes of achieving equality. Again, the point is that by not watering either stance down or finding a middle ground, the differences can continue to challenge each approach—no one becomes complacent.

Why was it important to leave these concepts "in friction"? Invoking the historical, personal and racialized legacies as they inform work in the community and beyond reflects what might be called the *story-behind-the-story* (Flower, 2008), the complex narratives that remain below the surface of immediately observable interactions but retain their power and influence. Excavating these narratives may pose a challenge when local institutions (possibly including universities) are seen as complicit in a racially charged and contentious past. In academic circles, calls for *engaged scholarship* will have to go both ways—we have to acknowledge first that the university needs to change; that expertise can and must always be challenged; and we have to continue to work toward our own personal processes of de-colonization as well as the de-colonization of higher education.

Co-authoring in the Versus: This is Writing

This book is just one example of the ways that we write, publish, and disseminate our findings publicly. Chapter 1 described the ways that collaborative writing is accomplished at our weekly writing group—an offshoot of the research team meetings. The dialogical processes that characterize our research practices also characterize our collaborative writing—generating new ideas, revising, and editing as we go. In addition to publications, the work has been presented, by various subsets of the whole team, at national and international academic conferences, as well as smaller venues such as the university and local churches. One of our first conferences involved the Freedom Market van, packed with seven researchers, from the community and the university, making its way from Rochester to Columbus, Ohio and back—rehearsing our presentation on the way there and critiquing what we'd seen at the conference on the way back.

The take-away here is that co-authoring in the versus, as we see it, is a practice of challenging epistemic injustice. It is an embodied practice of new epistemologies in which knowledge production is dialogically constructed, egalitarian, and distributed. What, then, is the role of the university in research? In issues of civic engagement, of social justice, and change? One of the foundational concerns of this project was to ensure that the benefits from public engagement would be distributed within the community in authentic and tangible ways. In other words, we had to resist simply relying on definitions of "beneficial" that looked good on paper only but have little "relevance" in the lives of participants (Gutiérrez & Penuel, 2014). For this project, bringing in the community perspective from the very beginning was non-negotiable. Full transparency is a necessity and obligation, not a generous gesture on the part of well-intentioned researchers. We suggest that in order to work against what might be seen as complacency on the part of isolated universities, and to foster a spirit of authentic partnership, hierarchies need to be challenged and extant assumptions about *whose knowledge counts* need to be deconstructed. Our approach provides one way of doing this—as researchers, scholars, and activists— we challenge each other to cross the boundaries of our comfort zones and roles. Moving outside expected roles or modes of interpretation can open spaces for new ways of thinking and being.

Discussion: Theory and Practice Our Way

The people, concerns, and ideas discussed above contributed to a complex blended model of theory and practice that developed over a year and a half of engaged effort, reflecting a uniquely relational approach to PAR (McIntyre, 2008), which involves critique and co-authoring alongside community residents (Cammarota, 2011; Flower, 2008; Kinloch, 2005, 2009). We started with the store as our site. Fourteen months in, we realized that the very idea of a single, specific approach or *site* was misleading, because we were dealing with a complex and changing network of places, persons, and interactions (as our rhizomatic Interdependence Model shows, see Chapter 2, Figure 2.2). Decades of groundbreaking work researching writing with communities provided a foundation for us, including Peck and Flower's Community Literacy Center and Kinloch's work in Houston and Detroit. But examples of this kind of authentically relational approach still remain scarce (Kinloch et al., 2016). The paradigm of university researchers studying community participants at a distance and with a time limit, and in which funding and publication are the ultimate priorities in decision-making, is still unfortunately the prevailing approach.

We used constructivist grounded theory (Charmaz, 2014) and followed a PAR-style cycle of data collection-analysis-implementation-collection in iterative cycles to build a local evidence base about community food, literacy, and family practices and to document the effectiveness of this project based on criteria that residents themselves determined. We implemented PAR in a way that made sense to the team, developing a process intended originally to benefit the store, but quickly expanding to generate new projects (see Chapters 6 and 7), new interpretive frames, new theories, and new research practices. Originally, we met only when a question or problem arose, and one team member took meeting "minutes." We found the dialogues so beneficial, we implemented a schedule of weekly meetings. Meetings were taped and transcribed. Transcriptions, along with field notes, were shared and discussed at meetings. This sort of recursive process allowed us to think through issues and return to them to develop emergent solutions. Through these processes we came up with seemingly small but effective changes. For example, it was decided that researchers would stop taking notes in the store, but rather work the register or clean and focus on really being there. It was also decided that quick updates about all the related side projects (the afterschool program and a community arts mural project, for example) would be presented at meetings, even if the whole team was not directly involved, so that everyone was aware of the big picture. Further, the group decided through this recursive process that we would implement bi-weekly writing group meetings—to keep the scholarship and publication processes active and dynamic—even if we did not have an upcoming conference or presentation. As a team we read and coded transcripts—debating and challenging each other about how a tiny code might be multiply and paradoxically interpreted (see Chapter 5 for a discussion of how the team grappled with the terms "soft" and "stand"—abstract concepts with immense importance on the ground). The implications of the work quickly exceeded the original questions and goals.

Conclusion

Our experiences speak to the idea that authentically engaged research needs to go beyond good will and a desire to help, and engage in ongoing, dialogic work at and across boundaries (Akkerman & Bakker, 2011; Akkerman & Niessen, 2012; Bakhtin, 1981). Our story and our work build upon and contribute to the growing foundation in community literacy work (Cammarota, 2011; Campano, 2007; Flower, 2008; Kinloch, 2005, 2009; Kinloch et al., 2016) that emphasizes research *with*—not *on*—communities. Framed this way, the work functions both to critique the status quo and to bring new social futures into current dialogue, reflecting Flower's (2008) definition of community literacy practice as "intercultural dialogue with others on issues that they identify as sites of struggles" (p. 19). In other words, to authentically practice transformative, dialogic research interventions, we all needed to think and work (and support each other, challenge each other, and argue with each other) as co-researchers, co-authors, and co-implementers.

We have found that once we stopped trying to "resolve" difference or "fix" tensions, and began to grapple with what they meant, these tensions became a source of energy—the play of difference fueled dialogue and ideas. In social-constructionist frameworks of collaborative knowledge-production, whether they call it "intersubjectivity," "intertextuality," or "dialogicality," cognition happens through interaction, and thinking and concept-building are seen as participatory endeavors (Ceci & Roazzi, 1994; Hutchins, 1995; Lave & Wenger, 1991;

Nasir & Hand, 2006; Nuñes, Schliemann, & Carraher, 1993; Rogoff & Lave, 1984). But a shared end goal does not necessarily equate to a shared understanding within processes themselves (Hanny & O'Connor, 2013; Larson, Webster, & Hopper, 2011). *That* sort of thing takes serious work. It seems to us that at least two significant and irreducible tensions or gaps inform learning and meaning-making, understood in these ways. First, there are tensions or gaps that characterize difference *between* participants. Engeström, Engeström, and Kerosuo (2003) note that "situated actions are inherently tension-laden, unstable and open-ended" (p. 287). Second, there are tensions and gaps that characterize difference *within* individuals, and these are brought into particularly stark relief in new and unfamiliar situations, for which we have no pre-existing conceptual framework or appropriate interpretive lens—in other words, pretty much any learning situation you can think of. This is where our diverse research team found itself—struggling to read each other as we learned to read the community.

One of our community members commented that the university seems to be "sleeping" and that the spaces that used to be the breeding ground of social action and change have become complacent. The sort of activism discussed in Chapter 1, in which radical dissent and protest were recognized by activists as justified and indeed necessary for change, seems no longer to hold sway in university discourses, increasingly shaped by marketplace ideologies and frighteningly conservative attention to the economic bottom line. We have attended conferences at which well-intentioned, activist faculty researchers expressed a desire to do this sort of collaborative work, and found that almost immediately, the conversation moved to concerns about budgets, funding, and tenure. A clear need exists, we would argue, to reinvigorate the notion of the public intellectual (Kinloch et al., 2016) and reinvest that role with a grassroots, community-minded energy. In a 2014 *New York Times* op-ed, Kristof put forth a call to universities and professors to not "cloister" ourselves like "medieval monks." He links the decline in public intellectuals with the cultures fostered in universities:

> a culture that glorifies arcane unintelligibility while disdaining impact and audience. This culture of exclusivity is then transmitted to the next generation through the publish-or-perish tenure process. Rebels are too often crushed or driven away. Where is the space for the public intellectual and the academics' incentive to fight and protest?

In our work, we are intentionally crossing traditional disciplinary and cultural boundaries. In the community, we find and feel ourselves "living in the versus" as we recognize the contrary discourses necessary for authentic engagement and sustainable change. This space we've co-constructed over many years, at the edge of our communities, this space of dissensus, has been accepted and embraced by us, our students, and our community team members.

However, we argue that we also need these spaces to wake up the university; we need to consider how we can explore "disrupting the university"; to open up new ways of thinking and being; to intentionally create spaces of dissensus across boundaries—the proliferation of creative new nodes. The small interactions described above suggest broader and wider new connections being formed over time and across contexts. Everyday democratic engagements emerge at the store, in front of the murals, at Freedom School, and at the new pizza parlor. But, as these examples, like the excerpts from research team meetings, show, democratic engagements and dialogic encounters should not be taken to suggest uniformity or consensus. Rather, we intentionally prioritize dissensus (Ziarek, 2001) and agonism (Laclau & Mouffe, 1985; Mouffe, 1993) as creative forces in our practice. These concepts are fruitful for understanding the importance of struggle and contestation that informs the work being done here. To responsibly consider learning and change practices within the store and the research team and beyond, we need to recognize the histories of the individuals, the community, and the sociopolitical sphere that are always at work. We have seen that addressing and making use of difference as generative frictions—rather than solving them or neutralizing them in the interest of group harmony or consensus—is a powerful way to move forward. We need to recognize the differences that inform our interactions and interpretations as a research team. These concepts from radical democracy, which see difference and struggle as generative, productive, and necessary for ethical political engagement, are far more effective for understanding the practices our study examines than are political models that foreground normative consistency or consensus building. To forget this is to risk complacency and foreclose meaningful change.

FIGURE 3.1 The stoop

We conclude this story of theory and practice in the versus at an entry point—the stoop in front of the Market. This threshold space is a natural gathering place for people to chat on their way in or out of the store, and for store personnel to get some fresh air. The threshold is a welcoming space—the store is a community hub inviting all. At the same time, the porch is a space that is watched over and in a sense protected. The store workers/community activists/researchers who have worked so hard to transform this space are vigilant about ensuring that negative messages around "hanging out" are not perpetuated on this site. On several occasions, individuals who engaged in unhealthy behaviors, creating a negative message to the community, have been asked (and at times strongly told) to leave the porch. In this way, the porch itself symbolizes an example of boundary crossing. The sort of dialogic encounters and democratic engagement fostered by the store and the research project are spaces of interaction, inviting difference—but they are also spaces in which respect is intentionally and assiduously protected. Attention to the fact that the community's next generation is watching and learning is never far from the minds of those who actively participate. How does one come to read the boundaries of the porch? How does one come to understand their role—as a teacher, learner, merchant, patron, expert, newcomer, elder, or researcher? We reflexively consider these questions as we engage in the very sorts of boundary crossing that dialogic, democratic interaction requires.

Earlier in this chapter we claimed that this story functioned as part of an intervention on three fronts. First, that it works to *challenge the power disparities* that characterize many university/community partnerships and the economic and social capital inequities they may mask. We hope that this brief history, and the remaining stories in this book, demonstrate that these disparities are prevalent, however deeply they may be buried, and that things can indeed be otherwise. Second, it contributes to a complex understanding of *literacy practices* as socially constructed, culturally relevant, and locally defined. We hope that this overview and the other glimpses of our work provided in this book will be read alongside powerful work that blends research and new literacies—learning within and alongside communities. Third, we claimed that our story *contributes to a powerful emerging force in research paradigms that prioritize authentic participatory actions and activism.* We hope this work serves as testimony to the possibilities and potency of work that takes seriously the charge put forth by Gutiérrez and Penuel (2014): that "rigor" in research should include a criterion of "relevance to practice" in "dynamic local contexts" (p. 19). It is time to close the chapter on research paradigms that ignore the meaningful and local complexities behind the surface-level facts or that devalue the wisdom and lived experiences of participants in the interest of academic gains of researchers.

On with the story …

References

Akkerman, S.F. & Bakker, A. (2011). Boundary crossing and boundary objects. *Review of Educational Research*, *81*(2), 132–169.

Akkerman, S. & Neissen, T. (2012). Dialogical theories at the boundary. In M. Märtsin, B. Wagoner, E. Aveling, I. Kadianaki, & L. Whittaker (Eds.), *Dialogicality in focus: Challenges to theory, method, and application* (pp. 53–64). New York, NY: Nova Science.

Bakhtin, M. (1981). *The dialogic imagination*. M. Holquist (Ed.), M. Holquist & C. Emerson (Trans.). Austin, TX: University of Texas Press.

Cammarota, J. (2011). From hopelessness to hope: Social justice pedagogy in urban education and youth development. *Urban Education*, *46*(4), 828–844.

Campano, G. (2007). *Immigrant students and literacy: Reading, writing, and remembering*. New York, NY: Teachers College Press.

Ceci, S. & Roazzi, A. (1994). The effects of context on cognition: Postcards from Brazil. In R.J. Sternberg & R.K. Wagner (Eds.), *Mind in context: Interactionist perspectives on human intelligence*. Cambridge, UK: Cambridge University Press.

Charmaz, K. (2014). *Constructing grounded theory: A practical guide through qualitative analysis* (2nd ed.). London, UK: Sage.

Curwood, S.E., Munger, F., Mitchell, T., Mackeigan, M., & Farrar, A. (2011). Building effective community-university partnerships: Are universities truly ready? *Michigan Journal of Community Service Learning*, *17*(2), 15–26.

Dempsey, S. (2010). Critiquing community engagement. *Management Communication Quarterly*, *24*(3), 359–390.

Engeström, Y., Engeström, R., & Kerosuo, H. (2003). The discursive construction of collaborative care. *Applied Linguistics*, *24*(3), 286–315.

Flower, L. (2008). *Community literacy and the rhetoric of public engagement*. Carbondale, IL: SIU Press.

Freire, P. (1998). *Teachers as cultural workers: Letters to those who dare to teach*. D. Macedo, D. Koike, & A. Oliveira (Trans.). Boulder, CO: Westview Press.

Fricker, M. (2007). *Epistemic injustice: Power and the ethics of knowing*. Oxford, UK: Oxford University Press.

Gutiérrez, K.D. & Penuel, W.R. (2014). Relevance to practice as a criterion for rigor. *Educational Researcher*, *43*(19), 19–23.

Hanny, C. & O'Connor, K. (2013). A dialogical approach to conceptualizations of residents in community organizing. *Mind, Culture, and Activity*, *20*(4), 338–357.

hooks, b. & West, C. (1999). *Breaking bread: Insurgent black intellectual life*. Boston, MA: South End Press.

Hutchins, E. (1995). *Cognition in the wild*. Cambridge, MA: MIT Press.

Kinloch, V. (2005). Poetry, literacy, and creativity: Fostering effective learning strategies in an urban classroom. *English Education*, *37*(2), 96–114.

Kinloch, V. (2009). Suspicious spatial distinctions: Literacy research with students across school and community contexts. *Written Communication*, *26*(2), 154–182.

Kinloch, V., Larson, J., Faulstich Orellana, M., & Lewis, C. (2016). Literacy, equity, and imagination: Researching with/in communities. *Literacy Research: Theory, Method, and Practice*, *65*, 94–112.

Kristof, N. (2014). Professors, we need you! *New York Times*. Retrieved from www.nytimes.com/2014/02/16/opinion/sunday/kristof-professors-we-need-you.html?mcubz=0.

Laclau, E. & Mouffe, C. (1985). *Hegemony and socialist strategy: Toward a radical democratic politics*. London, UK: Verso.

Larson, J., Webster, S., & Hopper, M. (2011). Community coauthoring: Whose voice remains? *Anthropology & Education Quarterly, 42*(2), 134–153.

Lave, J. & Wenger, E. (1991). *Situated learning: Legitimate peripheral participation*. New York, NY: Cambridge University Press.

McIntyre, A. (2008). *Participatory action research*. London, UK: Sage.

Mouffe, C. (1993). *Return of the political*. London, UK: Verso.

Nasir, N.S. & Hand, V.M. (2006). Exploring sociocultural perspectives on race, culture, and learning. *Review of Educational Research, 76*(4), 449–475.

Nuñes, T., Schliemann, A.D., & Carraher, D.W. (1993). *Mathematics in the streets and in schools*. Cambridge, UK: Cambridge University Press.

Postma, D. (2016). Open access and epistemic equality. *Education as Change, 20*(2), 2–10.

Rogoff, B. & Lave, E. (1984). *Everyday cognition: Its development in social context*. Cambridge, MA: Harvard University Press.

Shultz, L. & Kajner, T. (2013). *Engaged scholarship: The politics of engagement and disengagement*. Rotterdam, The Netherlands: Sense Publishers.

Ziarek, E.P. (2001). *An ethics of dissensus: Postmodernity, feminism, and the politics of radical democracy*. Stanford, CA: Stanford University Press.

4

FREEDOM AIN'T FREE ... BUT IT'S WORTH THE COST

George Moses, Ryan Van Alstyne, Jeremy Smith, Joanne Larson, Brittany Calvin

> If we are concerned about breaking down the power structure, then we have to be concerned about building our own institutions to replace the old, unjust decadent ones which make up the existing power structure.
> —*Charles Cobb, 1964*

We march. Following the notion of sankofa, or looking back to see the future, we begin this chapter by honoring the work of civil rights activists before us. During the civil rights movement, people marched. As George stated, "In a movement there has to be *movement*. At each milestone, you move to it. As you walk, you take the ground." When we marched from the Freedom School to the Market on opening day, it was an economic taking of the ground. We wanted the children to see the work of transforming the neighborhood as their accomplishment too. Thus, we moved from the Freedom School to the Market in parade fashion. We connected this geographic taking ground theoretically to Lefebvre's (1991) concept of taking back the city; in a very real way, Beechwood residents marched to take back the city and to access what Soja (2010) refers to as urban residents' spatial rights.

The questions that emerged while planning the march were: do we just march or do we march and celebrate? Part of how we answered this question was shaped by the bureaucracy of city hall. When we went to inquire at the relevant city office, they called what we wanted to do a "parade" when we suggested it was a celebration and they said we would need a permit. They established a waiting period that meant we wouldn't have been given the permit until after the day the parade was going to happen. We asked, "How else do you stop traffic?" A funeral! We sent Wallace and Joyce to a funeral home to get a hearse, but told them we didn't need it for a body. The funeral home wouldn't give us a hearse because no one was dead. In the end, George simply told the city that on that day, at this time, 100 plus children would be walking down the streets to open the store—deal with it. By the time the day arrived, the city had buses rerouted and we had a police escort. City officials, including the two candidates for Mayor and the city councilor for Beechwood, marched along with the Freedom School kids. News cameras documented the whole event. We had a truck with dance music accompanying the children as they danced in the street in front of the new Market. Sometimes you just have to take the city.

FIGURE 4.1 Freedom Market opening day (photographs by Adrian Alim)

The Freedom School children and youth also "took back" a neighborhood park that was extensively used by local drug dealers. One day, the Freedom School kids simply decided they wanted to play at the park. Upon seeing the children and their community marching toward the park, the dealers moved out of the way and gave the space to the kids. Each time the children came to play, the dealers repeated these actions, often nodding in acknowledgement to the incoming crowd.

We begin with the stories of taking back the city to illustrate the deep interconnection between history and the present and between the nodes of our Interdependence Model (see Chapter 2). We look back in history to understand the present and to plan for the future. Opening day at Freedom Market (see Chapter 5 for the Market story), provides the celebratory backdrop for our description of NEAD's Children's Defense Fund (CDF) Freedom School in this chapter. The Freedom School is a foundational node in the collaborative work we do in the Beechwood neighborhood. The Freedom School was one of the first initiatives NEAD established as they began the work of community transformation. We will describe how the Rochester Freedom School came about, what we have learned in the process, and how the Freedom School connects to all the spaces of our work.

The Rochester Freedom School Movement

Before telling the story of the Rochester Freedom School, it is important to understand what the Freedom School movement is and how it developed. Freedom Schools began during the Civil Rights Movement in the U.S. as part of larger goals for social, economic, and political freedom and education equity articulated by the Student Nonviolent Coordinating Committee (SNCC) (Perlstein, 1990). Following *Brown* v. *Board of Education* in 1954, many schools in the American South remained highly segregated and unequal. In 1963, Charles Cobb proposed a network of Freedom Schools as part of the development of Freedom Summer that would afford African American youth an opportunity to participate in civil rights organizing activities while also learning academic practices denied them in segregated schools (Perlstein, 1990; Sturkey, 2010). By the end of Freedom Summer, over 40 Freedom Schools operated throughout Mississippi using a curriculum based on principles of emancipation and focusing on developing academic skills (Emery, Braselmann, & Gold, 2004[1]). By 1995, the Children's Defense Fund sponsored Freedom Schools across the U.S. As of 2015, there were 189 Freedom Schools in 96 cities and 29 states.[2] As stated on the CDF website:

> The CDF Freedom Schools® program seeks to build strong, literate, and empowered children prepared to make a difference in themselves, their families, communities, nation and world today. By providing summer and after-school reading enrichment for children who might otherwise not

have access to books, the CDF Freedom Schools program plays a much needed role in helping to curb summer learning loss and close achievement gaps—and is a key part of CDF's work to ensure a level playing field for all children. In partnership with local congregations, schools, colleges and universities, community organizations, and secure juvenile justice facilities the CDF Freedom Schools program boosts student motivation to read, generates more positive attitudes toward learning, increases self-esteem and connects the needs of children and families to the resources of their communities.

NEAD built on these principles by adding the tenets of *nguzo saba* and theories about funds of knowledge (González, Moll, & Amanti, 2006) and culturally relevant pedagogy (Ladson-Billings, 1995) (see Table 4.1).

NEAD's Road to Freedom School

George and Ryan had been looking for ways to move past sporadic programs and achieve true neighborhood transformation for a long time. Looking for something that would work, they had been trying "programs" for years. Ryan found information about the CDF Freedom Schools and when they called, someone answered the phone! They applied to establish a Freedom School in Rochester and were accepted. However, they didn't have the funding to go for training. CDF kept in contact and when they had an expansion funded, CDF sent George an invitation to Haley Farm in Clinton Tennessee.[3]

As Ryan put it, "CDF sent for us." Both George and Ryan thought it was a joke at first. When the itinerary came they were still skeptical and because the airline AirTran was new to Rochester, they thought it was shady. It was a straight flight to Knoxville, TN. Someone greeted them holding a sign that read, "Haley Farm." There were a couple of other people at the airport who were there for the same thing so they started to feel like there really was something happening. They got on a bus with the others and drove to the middle of nowhere. In the middle of a road they approached a secure gate that needed a code to enter. People were looking at each other with deep curiosity, worrying about where they were.

Once inside the gate, they found the most beautiful place they'd ever seen. A crowd of African Americans and Latinx were chanting "Welcome home!" Hugs, chanting and sharing made them feel warm and accepted. Inside, the lodge and training center were cozy. The head chef came out asking if there was anything they wanted to eat. George and Ryan soon made friends with the cook and ended up being master taste testers during their stay. Since this first trip, NEAD has sent over 150+ "servant leaders" (college students) to Haley Farm for training.

The first iteration of Freedom School in Rochester was under Rose Washington at Berkshire Farms who matched the funding George received from NY State Senator Joe Robach. Along with Robach, key members of the staff at the Rochester Area Community Foundation were instrumental in securing additional funding and establishing a relationship with Janet Buchanan Smith (an individual donor from the Rochester Area Community Foundation) that continues today. However, the relationships with Berkshire Farms Center and Services for Youth soured due to internal politics. When George took his position at NEAD, the funding and positive relationships followed. They used three different church buildings to house Freedom School until John Page (then NEAD Executive Director) came one day and said, "Hey, I found a building for the school." NEAD purchased the dilapidated building in 2008. After extensive renovation supervised by John Page, who served as developer and construction manager, the Freedom School formally moved into the renovated building in 2007. Consistent with Mr. Page's lifelong vision and work in the community, some professional contractors were hired to do structural and framing work, however the bulk of the work was done in collaboration with community members. The building was dilapidated and being used as a chop shop. People were using the back area for drugs and to turn girls out for prostitution (see Figure 4.2). During the renovation, all these activities moved to abandoned houses next door, but over the years NEAD has fought to remove or purchase these houses. They are still fighting.

This work to rehabilitate the building is part of the larger goals of neighborhood transformation. NEAD's larger work in this area includes housing development, renovating a large building along one main street that now includes the Museum of Kids Art (MOKA), a respected child care center (Caring and Sharing Child Care Center), the Dazzle Theatre, a tool library, and a new franchised pizza parlor (Salvatore's Speedy Slice). These projects include extensive job preparation for area residents who are hired to do construction and to work in the different spaces. All of these initiatives comprise an overarching commitment to economic development and sustainability. Furthermore, these initiatives connect to the *nguzo saba* principles of *ujima* (collective work and responsibility) and *ujamaa* (cooperative economics).

The goal at the beginning of the Rochester Freedom School was to reduce summer reading loss. The leadership team called it the "war on illiteracy" and they wore fatigues, brown shirts, and army boots because they were dressed for war—a war of the mind. In the first summer 2008, the school served 189 students. They have remained consistent in serving 130–150 children and youth each summer, making an approximate total of over 2,400 since its inception.

Rochester Freedom School Methodology

The methods of the Freedom School are designed to foster growth in nine areas of socio-cultural learning, which have been found to be effective in increasing academic achievement with students of color (Allen & Boykin, 1992; Ladson-Billings, 1995). By providing experiences that connect academic learning with

FIGURE 4.2 The Freedom School: Before and after

the strengths families and communities offer, Freedom School incorporates the funds of knowledge that families bring to school (González et al., 2006) into the total school program. A key component of the program is building learning communities that offer a sense of safety, love, caring, and personal power that lead to transformative education. The program focuses on: (1) literacy, using culturally relevant high-quality books and materials; (2) encouraging children to dream, set high goals and expectations, and cultivate positive attitudes; (3) wholesome nutrition; (4) civic engagement and social action; (5) developing non-violent conflict resolution skills; (6) connecting families with health care and other resources; (7) engaging youth in music, cheers, and chants that have positive affirmations. The school works with youth to develop a positive life outcome. Table 4.1 illustrates the activities and curriculum principles used to achieve each of the program's nine areas of learning and the program's focus areas.

The principles of *nguzo saba* (unity, self-determination, collective work and responsibility, cooperative economics, purpose, creativity, and faith) are woven

TABLE 4.1 Curriculum principles

Nine sociocultural areas of learning	Rochester Freedom School methods
Positive self-concept and image	Demonstrate Heritage Knowledge as a framework for school-day and after-school programs (i.e. *Kwanzaa* principles).
Self-knowledge and appraisal	Teach cultural precepts such as "know thyself," "oneness/unity," and "balance and reciprocity" in the context of program activities.
Cultural excellence	Provide examples of cultural excellence that have been consistently demonstrated in diverse disciplines, as seen in books, films, and "live" presentations.
Effective navigation of the social system	Provide forums for discussing institutional racism and other group-based oppression, including internalized oppression.
Identification and pursuit of long-term goals	Foster the individual and collective idea that I/we can and must make a difference in myself/ourselves, family, community, school, country, and world.
Being mentored and mentoring others	Teach the intergenerational responsibility of mentoring. Everyone mentors those who are younger and is mentored by those who are older.
Leadership experience	Guide students in civic engagement projects in their communities and in developing the agency to take social action, using local and national examples of change-making movements.
Knowledge acquired in literacy	Engage parents, students, and community members in literacy activities related to families' funds of knowledge (e.g. book groups, poetry readings, music and literacy presentations).
Community engagement in curriculum and instruction	Engage teachers to experience what students and families have produced in literacy activities, and to discuss how to incorporate this knowledge into classroom curriculum and instruction.

© Rochester Teacher Center and Freedom Community Enterprises throughout the curriculum. *Umoja*, or unity, focuses on building and maintaining unity in the family, community, nation, and race. The emphasis on an asset-based, funds of knowledge perspective in the curriculum, along with the principle of *kujichagulia* (self-determination), which focuses on the community's right to define themselves, are echoed in the curriculum in multiple ways.

Interpreting the Freedom School using our conceptualization of developmental trajectories and transformational pathways (see Chapter 2), we trace entry points for members of our research team. While people enter through various pathways, we have come to see that building relationships is the primary pathway into our Interdependence Model. People "enter" the Freedom School community through relationships, both existing and new. Knowing someone or having a family member who tells you about Freedom School is a common entry point. Figure 4.3 illustrates when different people joined the Freedom School work, even though they also participate in activities across the nodes in the network.

For example, TaShara and Kim both began as parents of children in Freedom School's summer program. TaShara became a servant leader after training at Haley Farm, then a teacher in Freedom School while she obtained her Master's

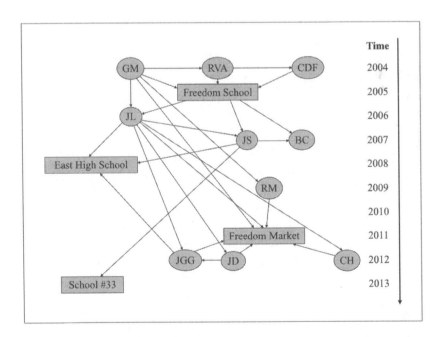

FIGURE 4.3 Freedom School relationship timeline

Note: GM – George Moses; RVA – Ryan Van Alstyne; CDF – Children's Defense Fund; JL – Joanne Larson; JS – Jeremy Smith; BC – Brittany Calvin; RM – Robert Moses; JGG – Joel Gallegos Greenwich; JD – Joyce Duckles; CH – Courtney Hanny.

degree and teaching certification. She is now teaching in a Rochester charter school. Kim's pathway was also through building relationships with Freedom School and NEAD staff as a parent. Her ability to develop strong relationships with parents and families led to her becoming Director of Family Relations for NEAD. What we see in these examples is entrance through the developmental trajectory of building relationships onto the transformational pathway from social justice to economic justice, which in turn builds on all seven *nguzo saba* principles.

Conclusion

Our description of NEAD's CDF Freedom School illustrates how relationships, community-determined principles, and participatory ethnography work together to produce new pathways for community transformation. This "hub" in our Interdependence Model constructs developmental trajectories and transformational pathways for youth and adults in Beechwood in ways that are socially, politically, and economically sustainable. The Freedom School has deeply impacted those who work and teach there and those who learn there. All of us on our research team feel like the Freedom School is a homeplace where we are nourished as we go about our activist work in this community and beyond. We have each other's back no matter what. Sometime that "what" can be overwhelming and painful. Making ourselves vulnerable to each other deepened our relationships but was often difficult. Sometimes one or more of us felt like we were out there alone. However, starting the day participating in Harambee[4] with over 100 children and youth inspires us to keep going. George, Robert, Wallace, and parents and families in the community all start their mornings at Freedom School by participating in Harambee. Joanne, Joyce, Joel, Courtney, and students or other university faculty also come for Harambee whenever possible. The time with children and youth, singing, dancing, and chanting centers their spirits on the work of transformation of self, family, community, country, and world. After Harambee, Robert and Wallace leave for the day's work at Freedom Market and George heads to his office across the street from the Market, or wherever the day takes him, re-energized for the day's work—we all move across and between nodes in our network, carrying with us the seeds of transformation begun so long ago. While freedom ain't free, the armed love or "the fighting love of those convinced of the right and the duty to fight, to denounce, and to announce" (Freire, 1998, p. 209) we garner from this work is "damn sure worth the cost."

Notes

1 See Children's Defense Fund (1998). *Rekindling the Spirit: A Vision for the New Millennial Movement to Leave No Child Behind* for deeper discussion of the history of the Freedom School movement.
2 For further information see www.childrensdefense.org/programs/freedomschools/.

3 For details of the CDF's resource at Haley Farm see www.haleyfarm.org.
4 Harambee is the opening celebration each day at Freedom School, consisting of singing, chanting, call and response, and a read-aloud. The concept originated in Kenya and refers to coming together before we go out and do the work.

References

Allen, B.A. & Boykin, A.W. (1992). African-American children and the educational process: Alleviating cultural discontinuity through prescriptive pedagogy. *School Psychology Review*, *21*(4), 486–596.

Children's Defense Fund (CDF) (1998). *Rekindling the spirit: A vision for the new millennial movement to leave no child behind*. Washington, DC: CDF.

Cobb, C. (1964). "Overview of the Freedom Schools," reel 68, frame 424, the Student Nonviolent Coordinating Committee Papers, 1959–1972, microfilm version, University of Michigan Research Collections, Ann Arbor, MI.

Emery, K., Braselmann, S., & Gold, L.R. (2004). Mississippi Freedom School Curriculum. Retrieved 2/16/17 from www.educationanddemocracy.org.

Freire, P. (1998). *Teachers as cultural workers: Letters to those who dare to teach*. Boulder, CO: Westview Press.

González, N., Moll, L.C., & Amanti, C. (Eds.) (2006). *Funds of knowledge: Theorizing practices in households, communities, and classrooms*. New York, NY: Routledge.

Ladson-Billings, G. (1995). Toward a theory of culturally relevant pedagogy. *American Educational Research Journal*, *32*(3), 465–491.

Lefebvre, H. (1991). *The production of space*. D. Nicholson-Smith (Trans.). Oxford, UK and Cambridge, MA: Blackwell.

Perlstein, D. (1990). Teaching freedom: SNCC and the creation of Mississippi Freedom Schools. *History of Education Quarterly*, *30*(3), 297–324.

Soja, E. (2010). *Seeking spatial justice*. Minneapolis, MN: University of Minnesota Press.

Sturkey, W. (2010). "I want to become a part of history": Freedom Summer, Freedom Schools, and the Freedom News. *The Journal of African American History*, *95*(3–4), 348–368.

5

WE ARE "ALL THE WAY LIVE"

Reading Community

*Joanne Larson, Joel Gallegos Greenwich,
George Moses, Robert Moses, Wallace Smith*

> I know there is strength in the differences between us. I know there is comfort, where we overlap.
>
> —*Ani DiFranco*

"Oh shit. Wallace just locked us in!" Joanne thought as Wallace stormed to the front door and locked it. Having just come in from the front of the store where he witnessed a young man buy drugs from an unknown person and immediately enter the Freedom Market, Wallace immediately yelled to the staff member working the register to push the security panic button that's installed for emergency situations and refuse to take the young man's money. Joanne was present at the Market for her weekly research observations. Within a half an hour of her arrival things went from celebrating young men dancing or "popping" outside the store, to being locked in and awaiting the arrival of the police. This was referred to as an "all the way live" day at the Freedom Market which translates to "you never know what is going to happen" on any given day inside the store. Part of what it means to do this work is to always be prepared to "stand" when unexpected events like this take place or even go in a more dangerous direction.

We use the story of this young man and Wallace, a community elder, to illustrate what we mean by community literacies and to show how people in one community read the word and the world (Freire & Macedo, 2013). We begin with the view of literacy as a set of multiple and changing social practices (Larson & Marsh, 2015; Leander & Rowe, 2006) that carry and shift across specific sites and persons within a complex "rhizomatic" web of relations. In this view, literacy is not simply what people do with written text, in other words, reading and writing in a traditional sense, but rather we see text as more than just words on paper. Texts include layout, font, image, sound, gesture, emotion, and cultural repertoires (Gutiérrez & Rogoff, 2003). From this perspective, people in communities read each other and texts in locally constructed ways. Being literate, as in knowing how to read and write at the Market, involves a set of practices that are intentionally co-constructed and then dialogically enacted across spaces and places in our community. We see all literacy practices as intentional in that they have audiences and purposes beyond the Market (e.g. rental agreements, flyers, legal documents). What might seem like unintentional practices (e.g. reading food labels) are used intentionally by Market staff as educational spaces while people interact at the Market. These practices are the foundation of community literacy practices, as multiple members of our community become co-constructors and participants of the spaces or "hubs" of interdependence (see Chapter 2).

Generative frictions, as described in Chapter 2, often produce dissensus, the process of growth and generativity that emerges from struggle or friction between people. Using Foucault's (1990/1978) analytics of power, which argues that where there is power there is resistance, we identified spaces of friction as power relations come into contact and found that these spaces were generative; power produces. We have witnessed this process in the Market whenever confrontation or a challenge results in deeper engagement between people. The story we tell in this chapter is an extreme example (but not rare) of a heated confrontation that involved a call to the police, yet the moment was still used purposefully to change attitudes and behaviors. The everyday reality in the store, however, involves more subtle and nuanced instances of purposeful generative frictions. Market staff deliberately cultivate these moments of friction as part of the shift from being a transactional space (exchange) to a transformational one. The practice of challenging assumptions, behaviors, and attitudes is part of what is valued as being a member of the Market family.

What Is the Freedom Market?

Building on the overall description of Rochester in Chapter 1, this section takes a closer look at the Beechwood neighborhood itself. Beechwood has approximately 6,000 residents with area challenges associated with concentrated poverty. According to 2015 data, Rochester ranks number one in the United States in terms of child poverty and in concentrated poverty among similar sized cities (Doherty, 2015). Beechwood has been a focus of citywide investment initiatives, which engage in strategic use of grant funds to leverage local resources and promote community revitalization, some of which NEAD has been able to access in its community work.

Initially, the Freedom Market took on the challenge of urban "food deserts" (Pothukuchi, 2005) and ubiquity of corner stores that sell high-priced, poor-quality foods. Food deserts are geographies common in high poverty urban areas marked by the absence of access to fresh food within a mile of homes.

McClintock (2011) suggests that food deserts disproportionately impact people of color and lower income neighborhoods and communities, where in many of these urban spaces there exists uneven community development and imbalanced relationships of power. Beechwood seemed to us to be more like a food swamp because it is inundated with unhealthy food.

Many residents do not have cars and must rely on public transportation to get around. While public transportation is an option for cheap and efficient mobility, it is not conducive to carrying several days' worth of groceries. One can take only a few grocery bags on a crowded city bus at any given time, forcing residents to select light, portable goods over heavier, cumbersome products (such as fruit and vegetables). To get to a full-service supermarket, residents need to take a taxi to the closest market, about a mile away. At approximately

FIGURE 5.1 The old Freedom Market

$10–15 per round trip, this takes a sizeable chunk of the household grocery budget, an option many households in the neighborhood simply do not have.

When NEAD purchased the Market in 2011, they closed on Friday and opened Saturday morning. It took more than a year to get started on the dramatic remodeling that needed to be done. The old store was dark, with heavy metal grates covering the windows and entry (see Figure 5.1). Signs for lottery, alcohol, and cigarettes littered the windows. The cash register was barricaded behind signs and food displays. And it was dirty. We spent days cleaning shelves and individual food items covered in dust even while the Market was open for business. Many expired items were thrown away. We removed the things that separated the cashier from customers and fought with tobacco salespeople to take down their signage. It took time, but while cigarettes and other tobacco products are sold, there is no evidence showing that they are—no tobacco signs and all such products are out of view. As of this time of writing, the Market is completely remodeled with new counters, coolers, and a prepared food counter with food cooked by residents in the newly installed kitchen. The space is clean and bright, has a new accessible ramp at the front door and, most importantly, there are no bars (see Figures 5.2 and 5.3).

FIGURE 5.2 Inside at the counter

FIGURE 5.3 New Market exterior

So What Happened to Joanne and Wallace?

Back to the emergency incident with Wallace. After the panic button was pushed, we all waited for the police to arrive. Wallace and the young man nearly got into a fist fight, but both were calmed down by a few customers in the store at the time. Joanne was struck by how calmly the customers reacted to the confrontation, evidenced by how they continued to engage in their routine transaction behaviors, which the research team felt reflected the phenomenon of normalized violence in their community. The young man pulled out his cell phone saying he was calling his parents. During this time, he removed his "thug" façade—put on to coexist safely in the community—to reveal a frightened child in need of his parents. Once the police arrived and put the young man in the back of their vehicle, Wallace started to tell the story of what happened. By this time, George had come across the street from his office at NEAD because he had "read" the situation from his second floor window. As a mediator in the partnership between the community and university, he had immediately thought, "Aw shit, they done locked our girl, Joanne, in the store during a code blue lockdown ... I hope she doesn't start screaming and cause another situation ... there goes our university partnership!" For George, reading the situation in that moment required an ability to negotiate his multiple roles as community member, gatekeeper of the community, partner of the university, and as Wallace's nephew. Wallace was still pretty agitated, but began to calm down as he recounted what had happened. George "read" Wallace, knowing his history as a Vietnam vet that has left a conflict legacy and knowing that talking about it would help calm him down. In standing up to the young man, Wallace claimed the new space and communicated that uncivilized behavior, such as using or buying drugs, loitering, and littering, would not be tolerated in and around the Market.

The young man's parents arrived quickly. Joanne could see that they were both very agitated as they came in the store looking for Wallace. After initiating handshakes with the parents, George and Wallace began to talk to them about what happened. The young man had pushed Wallace and treated him disrespectfully, not to mention the drug deal that took place outside of the store. The mother would hear nothing about her son doing anything illegal. They both started to walk away as the father said, "I'm done talking." But, after a few minutes, he came back without his wife. George, Wallace, and the father talked a few more minutes and before long the father went over to get the son from out of custody inside the police car. Joanne was impressed that the young man came back to the group of men, apologized to Wallace, and proceeded to ask for his forgiveness. It all happened in less than a half of an hour.

Meanwhile, what were the police up to? They could have arrived guns drawn and sirens blazing as is their typical response in this neighborhood. Instead, after putting the young man in the back of their vehicle without handcuffs, they walked into the store. One officer noted, "Hey, this is that store I saw on the news," as they gave themselves a tour of the store. They did not participate at all in the conversation George and Wallace were having with the parents. Contrary to current discourses about police behavior in predominantly low-income African American neighborhoods, these officers "read" the situation as being well in hand by neighborhood leadership (e.g. George). They had seen news reports about the Market working to change the neighborhood and also knew about NEAD's efforts to decrease neighborhood violence and illegal activities. They did not intervene to arrest the young man or to lead the reconciliation between Wallace and the young man's parents.

Reading this Scene

Viewed from our perspective of community literacies as "rhizomatic relations" across hubs of interdependence, each person read the social and cultural texts in this scene at the store from their point of reference. Wallace, an African American, read the scene from his perspective as a community resident, neighborhood elder, and store liaison. He saw the hand gestures and cash exchange that to him indicated a drug deal taking place. Someone else unfamiliar with this neighborhood or with what counts as a drug deal may not have read this interaction the same way. To Wallace, the drug dealing violated new cultural norms about the space in and around the store, so he reacted by trying to stop the young man from entering the store or from purchasing anything during the altercation and furthermore he called the police. As a community elder, he read the young man's physical challenge as disrespectful of elders and took deep offense to it. Joanne thought the young man must have been surprised at Wallace's strength (see Figure 5.4), previously unknown to the community (he's a Special Forces veteran). When "disrespectful force" was met with "absolute force" this might have contributed to the young man backing off. The reading of the combined violation of cultural norms (drug dealing and disrespecting elders) moved Wallace immediately into action.

Joanne read the scene from her perspective as a white woman and university researcher as a potentially violent situation that could go south quickly. Her experience of police interventions in African American urban neighborhoods shaped her worry that the police would escalate the situation beyond what was warranted. What will be important during later conversations, however, was that she did not panic or run away from the situation. In George's words, "you stood." Instead, she continued observing and taking some notes to make sure the event was documented—to be a witness to what happened. Even though she still jotted notes to bear witness, participating in the real life of the Market was also important. She stopped taking notes and moved outside after the family arrived to more closely observe the discussions and to be present if George needed anything, which, not surprisingly, he didn't. Her behavior was "read" by the community as a form of solidarity they are not used to from people outside of this community, white folks in particular.

The police read the situation, acknowledged and appreciated the intervention by key members of the community being there and talking to the family which meant to them that the situation was under control. We are not clear why the drug deal took a backseat to the disrespect of Wallace from the police's perspective; however, it was less about drugs than it was about a breakdown in communication about appropriate and acceptable norms in and around the Market space. The police did not arrest the young man, nor did they bring up the drug issue at all. Wallace did not press charges for what could have been read as an assault once the young man apologized. The Market offered a space for restorative justice practice, a principle used by George and the Market management and staff that focuses on restoring communication pathways that result in peaceful resolutions to conflict. This restorative space afforded time for discussion and reconciliation rather that arrest or criminality. **Banishment is not an option.** You have to address every situation as if the person is going to come back; how they come back will depend on whether the interaction is good or bad.

From his office window across the street, George (NEAD's executive director), observed that there was a situation that needed his immediate attention.

He watches the neighborhood from this office window every day and will come out to the street or to the Market whenever he feels his attention/intervention is needed, thus his nickname of "Brother man from the 5th floor." There is a normal sound the community has on any given day, you have to listen for the changes in tone that aren't the normal demonstrative speech. As George often says, "When you hear it start to boil, get on it and get on it quick." During this event, he heard Wallace's loud voice talking to the young man in the street and immediately read this as a potentially volatile situation. He was at the front door of the Market by the time the police arrived. He took charge of the conversation with the parents and, using restorative justice practices, he guided the conversation to a positive resolution.

Standing with the Community

The subject of what it means to "stand" came up again in a research team meeting and this story about Joanne's experience that day was used to discuss what it means to stand versus what it means to be "soft." In a key sense, the store incident produced a generative friction that activated the possibility to show how one should stand with community. About midway through the meeting, we began discussing some tensions that existed between community members and university researchers. The conversation moved to talk about standing with the community in what community members referred to as a "war zone." Residents on the research team, particularly Robert, often commented that the university members on the team went home to their safe neighborhoods at the end of the day. "The rest of us live here," he said. Standing with them given these important differences in geography seemed to mean dependability, or the confidence people would have that an individual would not run in a hostile situation, because "you never know what might jump off" at the Market or in the neighborhood. Trusting each other to stand together became a key marker of our relationships. Being able to "read" a situation and knowing whether standing is needed is an important community literacy in this context.

The following discussion came after one university researcher was challenged about what he meant when he said he was "soft." Following our thinking about how power produces generative frictions and dissensus, the conversation invoked an ongoing dissensus about this researcher's positionality. As an openly gay, biracial man, what he described as soft was often misinterpreted. The discussion below was what proved to be the end of this narrative thread once George clarified the community's worry about what the university researcher meant. Community members were reading the situation differently and wanted him to show whether he would stand in a fight. George led this part of the discussion and used Joanne's experience to illustrate what he meant by standing:

George:	Let me ask it in a different way.[1]
	I'm going to use your situation
	((looking at Joanne))
	we had an incident in the store
	>do you know<
	about the incident she had in the store
	((leans forward, looking at Tomás))
	where the gu:y
	had raised up on brother Wallace,
Tomás:	[Um yeah yeah
Joanne:	[Probably read about it in the field notes,
	there was a–
	Wallace locked us in
Robert:	((laughs loudly))
Joanne:	and the police came and there was–
	and George stepped i:n,
	it- it a:ll got resolved in a positive way,
George:	We didn't know what was going to happen in that situation
	and that situation will you sta:and
	or in that situation will a person
	start cryin and go crazy in the store=
Tomás:	[Oh I'm not going to do that=
George:	[then we got a–
	[We're talking about assault
Tomás:	=[I'm a professional– I'm a professional of course,
	right,
	but
George:	So that's what we're talking about
	you can't break–
	we understa:nd acro:ss the street
	is you in a– a war zone.
	It's all the way live
	it can go at any ti:me
	we don't even know
	what's going to ha:ppen
	when somethin go do:wn.
	So we got a situation that we have to mainta:in.
	and then if we got somebody who supposed to be with us,
	like you got a gun,
	((leans back in chair))
	I got a gun,
	we have battle
	and the battle start

	I'm shootin
	I look for you,
	you done ra:n off!=
Tomás:	((laughs))
George:	=So you got to see if a person is soft.
	Everybody goes through,
	we had to see what [you- was gonna to do.
	[((to Joanne))
	we saw she gonna sta:nd.
	We saw- y'all gonna sta:nd=
	((reaches hand toward Joyce))
Joanne:	((nods head))
George:	=We saw- I haven't seen yet-
	It looks like-
	we gotta see if you gonna sta:nd.
Tomás:	Yeah
George:	That's what we mean by soft.

This example illustrates how community members read the social text of the Market/neighborhood and strategically maintain their transformational goals. They are willing to stand with each other in any conflict to positively change the neighborhood. Anyone who collaborates in this effort has to show they can and will stand with the community. Tomás showed he would stand by showing up every day, no matter what. This is a crucial knowing upon which trusting relationships are built. This community has been betrayed by multiple outsiders who think they need rescuing. That "reading" happens in these kind of moments, when things "go all the way live," not in a rehearsed or planned way (see Chapter 6 for another similar moment). Knowing how to read these situations can sometimes determine your survival.

Generative Frictions

The analysis thus far has shown that generative frictions animate change. We saw in the Wallace story that the entrance of the young man from the street caused friction that generated a transformative event. George's articulation of what it means to stand with the community during a research team meeting uses potential frictions as starting points for showing one is not "soft." In both of these moments, the generative frictions produced deeper, more trusting relationships.

The process of generative friction is particularly evident in times when non-regular customers enter the Market. Because everybody in the Market is treated like family, it is easy to identify first-timers or non-regular customers when they enter the store. This excerpt from an interview with Rob speaks to the process of engaging first-timers:

You'll know who's not a part of everyday customer/merchant relationship because they don't speak, so you have to engage them, find them, meet them where they are, get them to where you want them to be by having those relationships where you speak and over time you'll be on a name to name basis. So the ones you know are regulars that come in and automatically speak because they know what the protocol is.

(Interview, 4/2013)

First-timers tend to act like customers in other stores who usually enter a store, pick up their products, pay for them, and leave without having engaged in any meaningful conversations. At the Freedom Market, however, first-time customers may enter as strangers and leave as family. Staff members make an intentional effort to ask customers questions relevant to their stage in life. For example, young people are asked about their school, parents are asked about their children, and so forth. Customers leave with the understanding that the Freedom Market is not only a space to buy products—it is a space to engage in meaningful conversations and to build trusting relationships (Memo, 4/2013). In this way, the Market moves away from simply being a transactional space towards being a transformative space. As relationships take hold and deepen, different community members move into other spaces (e.g. become Market employees, parents at the Freedom School).

During our data analysis, we found an interesting pattern concerning first-timers or non-regulars entering into the Freedom Market. When these

FIGURE 5.4 Wallace Smith

We Are "All the Way Live" 75

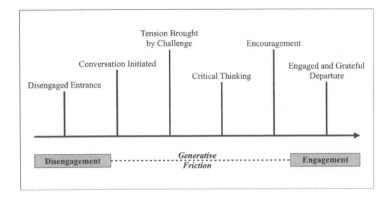

FIGURE 5.5 Generative frictions with Market first-timers

customers enter the store completely disengaged from the people around them, they enter the store with a single mission, which usually involves the purchase of a store product—a transaction. Then, one of the staff members (usually Wallace; see Figure 5.4) engages them in conversation. During the conversation, the staff member challenges the customer to think more critically on a particular topic of the conversation. The customer is challenged to think for themself. The tension brought about by the challenge is immediately followed by encouragement and positive reinforcement. The customers, then, leave the store expressing their gratitude. In short, the pattern looks something like this (see Figure 5.5):

1   Disengaged customer enters into the store;
2   Staff member engages the customer in conversation;
3   Customer is challenged by conversation;
4   Customer responds to challenge through critical thinking;
5   Customer receives reinforcement/encouragement from staff member;
6   Engaged customer leaves expressing gratitude.

Each step of the process of generative friction can be seen during this interaction between two young customers and Gregory (a Market employee) that Joel documented during an observation:

> At this time, two African American males who appeared to be teenagers walked into the store. Wallace greeted the boys, but they walked passed him without acknowledging him. He said, "Hold up!" and called the boys back to him. They walked back to Wallace reluctantly, evidenced by their slow walk and their heads dropping backwards. Wallace told them that he had a treat for them if they could tell him what they learned in school that day. Immediately, the boys stood up straight and started sharing about their day.

One student shared that he learned about a man named "Truman Harris" who made the decision to drop an atomic bomb on Japan. Wallace repeated, "Truman Harris?" The student, then, remembered the correct name, Harry Truman. Wallace asked him what Harry Truman's occupation was at the time. The boy said that he wasn't sure and that all he knew was that Harry Truman was a president who ordered an attack on Japan. Wallace said with a smile, "What do you mean by 'you don't know.' You just answered the question. Harry Truman was the president!" Another student said he learned about Gandhi in school. Wallace was pleased by hearing Gandhi's name, evidenced by his smile and his follow-up comment. He told the student that Martin Luther King, Jr. studied Gandhi's tactics of civil disobedience. Wallace, then, brought the treat basket up to the counter so that the boys could select a treat. While they were doing so, Wallace asked them if they would like to see a card trick and asked me to pull out my deck of cards. They agreed, so I showed them a couple of magic tricks. They thanked Gregory and me [Joel] and left the store.

(Field notes, 3/2013)

In a later interview, Wallace shared that when first-timers, such as the boys described in this excerpt, return to the store, they enter with a completely different understanding of the Freedom Market setting. Wallace said, "[I]t's become so repetitive that it's become a behavior in the children that you want to be replicated over and over again" (Interview, 4/2013). They adjust and change their behavior, which is a prime example of literacy as a social practice. In other words, rather than re-entering the store as disengaged customers, they enter with the expectation of engaging in a meaningful conversation, even if only for a few seconds. They are learning how to be in the Freedom Market setting. In this way, they come to understand what it means to be literate in this community—how to "read" each other and the world.

Conclusion

The generative pattern illustrated in Figure 5.5 shows how points of friction or conflict can activate transformative change. This process occurs in the store in everyday interactions (new customers learning store norms) and in more dramatic events (Joanne's experience in the store). Generative frictions also occur in the research team as we analyze data, discuss different theoretical positions, and come to understand what it means to "live in the versus" (see Chapter 3). We understand the connection between our rhizomatic model and generative frictions by seeing how generative frictions activate movement within and between the nodes in our Interdependence Model. A moment of friction, such as inappropriate education for African American boys in Rochester, generated the after school program at a nearby elementary school. Learning that the

Rochester City School District graduates only 21% of African American boys (Beaudry, 2015) generated our new work at a local high school (both schools constitute the "school" node in our model described in Chapter 6). Moments of friction within our research team have repeatedly served as catalysts to build trust with one another.

We live in a world of difference, and we should be grateful for that. Unfortunately, we seem to be programmed by society to react to our differences with fear, apprehension, or neglect. We label each other and build walls to distance and protect ourselves. In the age of computers, smartphones, and quick fixes, it is possible for us to be in each other's presence for hours at a time and never actually connect. We have heard time and again that the pathway toward community transformation is building relationships. And yet, it seems that we are doing an awful lot to avoid each other. One of the greatest causes for concern in today's society is our deep-seated addiction to comfort. Comfort is inherently incompatible with relationship building; indeed, the two cannot authentically coexist. Though our pursuit of comfort may offer us instant gratification in a variety of forms, it ultimately deprives us of opportunities to demonstrate empathy towards one another across difference and to negotiate creative solutions to interpersonal and systemic problems. Our work together at the Market and across the multiple nodes has shown that building relationships and "standing" actually involves facing, embracing, and leaning into moments of friction. It requires hard work, time, and presence. Unless we are willing to experience some discomfort—some friction—we will never be able to experience growth and generativity. As George has said, "Until you get into a conflict, you are talking to a representative." Here's to building relationships—that unpredictable, turbulent, and sometimes explosive process that allows us to reach our interpersonal and communal potential in which we are "all the way live."

Note

1 Transcription conventions for research team meetings are adapted from Atkinson and Heritage (1984) as follows: Colons denote sound stretch (sta:nd); underline denotes emphatic stress (person); brackets indicate overlapping speech; inward facing arrows indicate faster speech; equals signs denote that the second speaker immediately speaks without any pause or that they are interrupted but continue to speak, and commas indicate rising intonation.

References

Atkinson, J.M. & Heritage, J. (Eds.) (1984). *Structures of social action*. Cambridge, UK: Cambridge University Press.

Beaudry, A. (Ed.) (2015). *Black lives matter: The Schott 50 state report on public education and Black males*. The Metropolitan Center for Research on Equity and the Transformation of Schools at New York University. Retrieved from: http://blackboysmatter.org.

Doherty, E. (2015). *Benchmarking Rochester's poverty*. Rochester, NY: Rochester Area Community Foundation and ACT Rochester.
Foucault, M. (1990/1978). *The history of sexuality: An introduction*. New York, NY: Vintage.
Freire, P. & Macedo, D. (2013). *Literacy: Reading the word and the world*. New York, NY: Routledge.
Gutiérrez, K. & Rogoff, B. (2003). Cultural ways of learning: Individual traits or repertoires of practice. *Educational Researcher, 32*(5), 19–25.
Larson, J. & Marsh, J. (2015). *Making literacy real: Theories and practices in learning and teaching* (2nd ed.). London: Sage.
Leander, K. & Rowe, D. (2006). Mapping literacy spaces in motion: A rhizomatic analysis of a classroom literacy performance. *Reading Research Quarterly, 41*(4), 428–460.
McClintock, N. (2011). From industrial garden to food desert: Demarcated devaluation in the flatlands of Oakland, California. In A.H. Alkon & J. Agyeman (Eds.), *Cultivating food justice: Race, class, and sustainability* (pp. 89–120). Cambridge, MA: MIT Press.
Pothukuchi, K. (2005). Attracting supermarkets to inner-city neighborhoods: Economic development outside the box. *Economic Development Quarterly, 19*(3), 232–244.

6

LIVING UP TO THE PROMISE

School Connections

Jeremy Smith, Joyce Duckles, Joanne Larson, Robert Moses

The Story

An incident occurred at East High School—one of the urban schools in our Interdependence Model—the day before one of our research team meetings. The retelling of this story at the meeting that day happened when Jeremy's emotions were still raw, and when issues for the youth and community were still unresolved. We decided to put in Jeremy's words as they were said that day rather than turn what he said into academic language. We did this intentionally to give readers a picture of the Jeremy we know—passionate, dedicated, emotional, and real. We know this to be Jeremy's "crisis voice." Each of us has a crisis voice that comes out when things are "all the way live" (see Chapter 5). Part of our choice to do it this way is to let readers into our spaces of vulnerability; the spaces we show each other because of the years we have spent building trust and love for each other. Here is what he said:

> *I'm supposed to be on my way headed for 33 School and I get the call. I call George I can't go to this, I got to go over to East for one of our kids. I got to handle that. So I fly over to East, and as I'm flying over to East one of the students who were so-called caught up in the incident, he's walking away from the school, so I pulled over to the side. Yo bro, what's going on, why you up here, I just told you to go home. He's like, yo Mr. Smith, it wasn't even like that. Blah, blah, blah… I was just up here getting my track papers, I wasn't trying to run track. He gave me the track papers, he validated that. I said, okay, where you going now. He said I'm going home with my homeboy. Alright, go home, don't go back to East I'll talk to you tomorrow, he walks off.*
>
> *So now the student who was pulled off the bus. As I was driving a little bit more, across from the VOA [Volunteers of America] I see them at the corner at*

McDonald's with a girl. So I'm okay, well there was an incident and all the kids are walking away from the actual scene, so now I pull to the side and I'm talking to him. Yo, your name was specifically said as the one who started the fight, what's going on? We was about to fight but it didn't get to that, they told us to get off the campus, we were trespassing, so we were leaving the campus. It's over with, whatever, whatever. I'm like, you being up here, it's not going to solve anything. Whatever situation you have with any individual leave that there, it's in the past. You coming up here you are trespassing, and they will arrest you. You need to go home. I was like the cop just called me and they told me they was about to arrest you. So, I'm trying to show him how serious this is. He was like, oh, it ain't even like that, I'm leaving right now, I'm going home. I was like, how you getting home. He was like, I'm going to catch the bus. Have you got any money on you? He was like, no I ain't got nothing. I gave him five dollars. I even told the girl, please make sure he gets home and not more trouble. She was like, okay I promise, I'll make sure I do it.

We're done, he's walking toward the bus stop. I kid you not, not even 30 seconds later three cop cars swarm. So I'm getting in my car getting ready to leave. I couldn't even get into the car because I hear him—"Mr. Smith, yo Mr. Smith." So I'm like, oh my God, so I get out of the car, go over there and go yo, what's going on? So now the cop, the cop at East High, he took it upon himself to say like, oh yeah, he want to be a tough guy, we're going to arrest him. I'm like, for what? I was like, I just got done talking to him, he's okay, he's leaving the premises, he's not starting any fights, it's all good. What's the issue here? He's like, oh yeah, yeah, it's disorderly conduct. I'm like, disorderly conduct? What code? I'm like, what code is that, when can you not talk back to a cop? I can see if he was saying threats, he's not saying threats at you, he's not trying to inflict physical harm, so where is it having a conversation or disagreement says it's disorderly conduct?

The police officer told Jeremy that the youth had been at school looking for a fight. Jeremy explained to him that the youth had been there getting eyeglasses from the Vision Care program, and that he had been escorted by a Freedom School teacher. Yet, it was the case that words had been exchanged between the young man and other students, but there had been no fight. The student had been disrespectful toward the officer, but there had been no fight. Moreover, given the police officer had taken over the situation, his interpretation ruled the day. There was nothing East administration could do after this occurred. It was clear that this officer did not have a relationship with NEAD as did the officers we discuss in Chapter 5, who trusted that George would de-escalate the crisis.

We realized immediately when we began to reflect on this incident that this situation could have gotten worse very quickly. This was a moment of crisis that we needed to unpack while also modeling how to resolve crisis moments for the youth we work with who often do not have the resources to resolve conflict positively. We admonished the youth saying that when you are in a situation that is out of control, you have to control yourself. We acknowledge that the youth should not have exchanged words with the officer. And we realized his confrontation with police could have resulted in Jeremy's own arrest. This was also a concern for East administration as they observed the incident. Jeremy continues his retelling:

> *So what fight happened earlier in the day? So I'm confused about why they were so eager to put him in handcuffs, and I said to the cop, putting kids in handcuffs that transpires down the road five or ten years from now, that boy may psychologically be on him that you know what, maybe handcuffs is what I need to be in. There's a statistic out there that says that the more you put kids in handcuffs, the more down the road they tend to be either inmates or put in prison for a long time. So my thing is if you just talk it out with him about what he did was wrong and let's do that right here, now here on Main Street. You don't have to put him in handcuffs or nothing. We can do this right here.*
>
> *As I'm talking to him, the other two cops are proceeding to put him in handcuffs. I'm like, come on mister, what's this going to do? This ain't going to solve nothing. I'm like, this is pitiful man. I'm like, are you kidding me right now? This is pitiful. So we're arguing, so I'm arguing saying this makes no sense. I'm like, are you serious right now, this makes no sense, what are we doing to our young Black and Latino males right now?*
>
> *So after that whole melee happened, both sides calmed down. Me and the cop we apologized for being energetic toward each other. Let him go, nothing serious you know what I'm saying, it's over with.*

The youth was given an appearance ticket and assigned a public defender. However, he was not taken downtown to the police station. Instead, the police took him back to the high school. When teachers and staff, including Joanne, came out of the building, they told Jeremy and the youth they were not permitted at the school, that they were "trespassing." Jeremy noted that he thought they were East High students, but was told that while they were technically, they could not be at school without an escort. They were accused of coming up there, starting fights, and "causing havoc." We have since learned that *anyone*—youth, parents, even staff—who refuses to leave the building when requested to do so is determined to be trespassing; it was not a matter of being an East student or not. The police officer was adhering to this school district policy.

The generative frictions produced in this incident centered around the newness of this partnership and confusion around policies about students from different buildings being at East, whether or not they were technically enrolled at East. One such policy states that students at the other off-site option for East students must be escorted when coming to the building. This friction also produced a rethinking of how Freedom School kids were viewed at East. School counselors and staff spent more time at Freedom School and advocated for those who completed the program to walk in the district's summer school graduation ceremony, which was against central office policy. As we explain later in this chapter, the University of Rochester (UR) East Educational Partnership Organization (EPO) operated as a district within a district and did not follow central office policies for everything. During this transformative time, there were a lot of confusing situations. The East administration persisted with central office and our students walked in the ceremony. East has now decided to hold all graduation ceremonies in our own building so that all East students who graduate or complete the Freedom School program can "walk the stage."

Narratives of "Urban" and "Urban Youth of Color"

As our research team talked through the incident of the previous day, it seemed to us that the youth were being seen by the police officer as "causing havoc" and deserving of being put in handcuffs. They were viewed as "trespassers." Master narratives surrounding both "urban" communities and "urban youth of color" wove through the retelling of this one incident, echoing the ways Freedom School staff believe that these discourses have become systemic and entrenched in many of the practices in our schools and community.

Many researchers have uncovered and explored the evolution of these narratives and called for them to be interrupted. Kinloch (2007) proposed that contradicting stories are often juxtaposed with one another to give them power. "Urban" and "inner-city" invoke images of decline, collapse, and crime, whereas gentrification and suburbanization represent rehabilitation and safety. Kinloch demonstrated the ways in which these urban narratives are "often publicized as dangerous, criminal and nefarious in juxtaposition with conditions that are experienced as positive, culturally rich and participatory" (p. 61). Master narratives of urban high schools and Black and Latinx students follow similar patterns (Harper, 2015). The schools are viewed as "large, overcrowded, dark and dangerous" (p. 140) and the youth and families as apathetic, underachieving, and violent. The work to change this narrative about East and its off-site programs like Freedom School has proved to be difficult.

The experiences of urban adolescence/ts become interwoven into competing narratives as well. Groenke et al. (2015) presented the assumptions of independence, resistance and romance embedded in discourses of the Western adolescent. However, they argued that:

> these discourses—and their attendant definitions of "normalcy" for teenagers—get unevenly distributed for youth of color. As an example, when youth of color "resist" or "rebel against" the status quo in or outside of school, they become criminals—"public enemies," "menaces to society" …. Thus, youth of color don't truly get to be adolescents. Instead, when they enact the discursive roles available to (some) youth, they are viewed as deviant and abnormal, as sub-human.
>
> *(p. 36)*

As part of our work as a collaborative research team, we asked: Who gets to frame the narratives and tell the stories of our urban communities and urban youth? Can they be reframed through the telling of counter-narratives? Are there spaces for pushing back? We continue to work with East administration to redefine the deficit narrative about our youth as our collaboration with East continues.

Within our local context, these master narratives persist. The Schott Report in 2012, "The Urgency of Now" (Beaudry, 2015) ranked our city school district as the lowest in the nation for graduating Black and Latino males. In fact, our city was found to be graduating fewer than one in ten of our young men of color. At first, many in the city, in academic communities, and in the towns and villages surrounding our city responded with shock. However, they also accepted that these numbers must and could be accurate. Academics co-opted the statistics as rationales for school reform and increased funding for research. Community development organizations in the city pushed up their sleeves and created supports for families and youth, continuing the work that needed to be done. The numbers were challenged and revised; however, the current report, *Black lives matter: The Schott 50 state report on public education and black males* (Beaudry, 2015) reported our 2011–12 cohort graduation rate of black males at 21%. In 2015, our district claimed a rate of 46% graduating, 22% dropping out, and 38% "still in school" (NYSED, 2015).

The Schott Foundation website introduced their 2015 report by stating:

> For over a decade, the Schott Foundation's efforts to collect and publish national data on the four-year graduation rates for Black males compared to other sub-groups has been to highlight how the persistent systemic disparity in opportunity creates a climate and perception of a population who is less valued.
>
> *(www.blackboysreport.org, 2015)*[1]

One of the primary purposes of our collaborative research is to uncover and document how the young men and women in our community have been positioned as "less valued" and some of the ways the community is working with the youth to push back and create spaces for different narratives, novel identities and new pathways to emerge.

In this chapter, we trace three initiatives undertaken by NEAD/Freedom School to partner with East High both before and after the UR East EPO partnership to address the needs of youth who were not succeeding within the traditional educational setting. There are many lessons we have learned from the mistakes we made as a neighborhood organization trying to make authentic change in our community. We explore what happened when community took the lead, adopted a different mindset grounded in the Freedom School model, and worked together to intentionally reframe narratives and co-construct generative spaces to create alternative developmental pathways for our youth. Through this intense and intentional work, both the community and the youth are "living up to the promise."

History and Context

The UR Freedom–East program builds on a rich history of collaborative initiatives between NEAD, as a community-based organization (CBO), and East High School, the largest high school in Rochester and the school a large number of Beechwood youth attend. These programs emerged from the particular passion of this CBO to address the needs of the students and families in our community who are struggling within our schools and traditional systems of support. The holistic framework that frames the Freedom Schools, embodying the sociocultural pillars and the principles of *nguzo saba* (see Chapter 1), has informed all of these collaborations. Through each, NEAD has applied the Freedom Schools model (see Chapter 4) to support youth who were not "succeeding" based on school measures, with low grade point averages, high rates of suspension, low rates of school attendance, and high incidence of grade repetition. At one point, the school district identified these youth as "over age, under-achieving." In this chapter, we present an overview of three initiatives between NEAD and East High School, spanning from 2008 to our current program. Our goal is to trace these initiatives, framed and presented within a community mindset, and to share the lessons we learned. This historical and local perspective provides insights into the challenges we have encountered in our efforts to support youth who have not found success in the current pathways through school in our community, the ways that we have intentionally crafted alternative developmental and transformational pathways for these youth and their families, and how, together with youth, we are developing powerful counternarratives of strength, pride, and success.

East–Freedom Connection: Round #1

In 2008, a local city website reported on the "East–Freedom School," a collaboration between NEAD Freedom School, a vibrant summer and after-school program (see Chapter 4), and East High School of the Rochester City School District. The article, titled "Life Lessons at the New 'East–Freedom School,'" began with the story of a student, Irma, who had been struggling with school attendance and was feeling disillusioned and disconnected from school. Irma explained, "we had to deal through a lot (last year) ... My mom had to go and try to look for food for us and, you know, suffering." Her mom, Irma, and her three sisters had gone from Rochester to Florida and back again, staying with friends. The sisters were separated at times, and attending school was difficult for all of them.

The collaboration began with East High agreeing that they would give NEAD a list of potential students, kids who were struggling with attendance (both attending school and actually going to class). NEAD Freedom School was identified as a "satellite site" or "smaller learning community" by the East administration at that time. East was establishing a junior high, but some of the 7th and 8th graders were not flourishing in the high school environment. With the list of students, NEAD staff began recruiting families by going door to door. As a community-based organization, this practice of going into the community to find, talk with, and connect with families has always been part of their practice. Some of the families were difficult to find. Irma's sister, Liz, was the original name on the first cohort list of students and was one of the most difficult students to find. Through numerous contact leads and old addresses, the NEAD team finally found the family living in a homeless shelter. As they worked toward enrolling Liz in East–Freedom, they offered community support services to the family. Through their efforts, they found out that Irma was not attending school either.

Irma enrolled in East–Freedom School late in the fall of 2008. About 30 students attended school at the Freedom School with two certified teachers from East, University of Rochester student teachers, and the extensive support of the NEAD staff with their training in the Freedom Schools model and practices. Building on a key tenet of the Freedom Schools, connecting the needs of children and families to the resources of their communities, George approached Irma's challenges through a holistic framework. He was quoted in the article; "At some point someone has to say, let's stop and let's help the parent. Let's stabilize the family so that the family can have the young folks focus on school." Getting to the roots of the problem often meant going into homes, problem-solving along with families, and finding meaningful supports. East–Freedom was able to partner with other agencies to find Irma's family a home and bring their family together again. Irma and her sisters were able to focus on school, and as Irma said, "Now I feel better because now when I go to school, it's all about school right now."

The East–Freedom School served two cohorts of students over two years. Analyses of data demonstrated increased parental involvement, reduction of youth violence, increased scores on academic assessments, high attendance rates, and significant decreases in summer reading loss. Several indicators were particularly salient. During the year prior to attending East–Freedom 57.1% of former 6th graders and 90% of former 7th graders had been suspended. During our partnership program, 10% of each group were suspended. Absenteeism significantly decreased. Former 6th graders had a mean rate of 18.62 days absent, while former 7th graders had a rate of 107.10 days. These rates decreased to 3.47 and 10.0 for these cohorts. In fact, by the second marking period, 35% of 6th graders reached honor roll and 10% reached high honor roll. For the 7th graders, 20% earned honor roll and 20% high honors. Parental and familial involvement began with oaths of rededication, with parents rededicating to do whatever it takes for their children. The rates and levels of family engagement increased more than twofold across all groups.

Some families with youth about to enter the junior high also found out about the East–Freedom program. The word was getting out about the success that students were experiencing at the Freedom School, and families were concerned about their kids entering a traditional high school environment. The parents wanted a smaller learning community, and were able to enroll them in our program. These kids and their families flourished at East–Freedom.

In 2010 the program was ended. As a staff member explained:

> It was a change in principals at East. The previous principal told us the third year that our contract was up for question. When the new principal came in, they determined that NEAD's contract would be ended. They wanted to get those services for kids "in house" rather than outsource it to a community organization.
>
> *(Interview, 2012)*

In spite of the relatively short duration of this program, the impact on the developmental trajectories of many students demonstrated the strength of the Freedom Schools model for supporting youth who many had labeled "at-risk" in terms of their academic, social, and emotional pathways. The support of community members as staff and mentors, the attention to supporting families as well as children, the training in leadership and focus on literacy, and the culturally relevant curriculum and practices of the school generated motivation to read, learn, and succeed for youth and their families. This is how the families defined success. We continue to support them in meeting these goals while also reigniting their motivation to get a diploma, General Education Degree (GED), or to start a career. Many of these families continued to attend the Freedom Schools summer program, and several of the parents have become active agents of change in our community.

East High–NEAD Collaboration with Step-Up: Round #2

Although data had been collected throughout the East–Freedom program, NEAD staff learned the value of expanding documentation beyond test scores and frequencies to include qualitative analysis of the ways families and youth were navigating the systems of education and the challenges and strengths of their communities. In December 2012, we entered into a new agreement with East High. Once again, we were tasked with bringing our holistic approach to supporting youth who were struggling to succeed within the current school structure. Once again, we built on the Freedom Schools model and our team's broad expertise in education, community building, and family engagement.

We entered into a collaboration with staff of the "Step-Up Program" at East High, a new program designed to address the learning needs of youth who were labeled as "over-age, under achieving." The 76 "Step-Up youth" had previously not passed 8th or 9th grade, and were being provided with extra periods at the end of the day to work toward credit recovery and passing current classes. The school wanted to reach out to families; however, the school personnel did not have the time or manpower to go into homes. East High contracted with NEAD to work with the families of these youth. We had also begun our collaborative research with the University of Rochester and NEAD by then, and this team easily transitioned into these new waves of data collection and analysis. Our contract began in December 2012, giving us six months to work with families to "increase family engagement" and, in turn, impact school attendance and achievement.

The stakeholders in this program—community members, school personnel, and parents—all came together with the common belief that families are central to youths' development, that parents are the true experts on their children and their lives. One of our key roles was to reach into the homes of the Step-Up kids to encourage family engagement in school and to understand, more broadly, the strategies and processes families were adopting to navigate their everyday lives, their supports, and their constraints. Our focus on families is embodied in the Freedom Schools model, and is also embedded in research in school reform, which has provided compelling evidence of the potential of family–school–community initiatives to transform low-performing schools (Weiss, Lopez, & Rosenberg, 2010).

Our approach was designed to be iterative, to capitalize on the strengths of community activists and our collaborative research team to create a framework for:

- *Documenting* how parents interact with their homes, communities and schools;
- *Recognizing* that families interact with institutions and schools in multiple ways;
- *Validating* the strategies and resources that families were adopting as they engaged with their children and communities that fostered positive outcomes;
- *Building supports* that built on family practices that are contextually situated, culturally relevant, and sustainable.

In their report to the National Policy Forum, Weiss et al. (2010) put forth family, community, and school engagement as a strategy to support school success. This integrated approach is consistent with our Model of Interdependence (see Chapter 2), building on our knowledge that a "full spectrum of society's resources" are demanded to support all students, especially those who have been positioned and labeled as "disengaged." We view community members as key resources, both in the cultural capital they possess and the social capital they can access (Emerson, Fear, Fox, & Sanders, 2012). We also turn to studies of neighborhood effects (e.g. Burton & Jarrett, 2000; Furstenberg et al., 1999) that demonstrate the role of families in the ways that urban environments impact the development of youth. In fact, "family-level variables tend to be more strongly associated with child outcomes than neighborhood variables" (Leventhal & Brooks-Gunn, 2000, p. 325). Parents have been found to be the most effective mediators and moderators of neighborhood effects. However, we are still working on learning about the processes, domains and pathways by which this influence takes shape.

As we considered the local ecologies of the youth and families in the Step-Up program, our conceptual framework and review of the literature led us to:

- *Learn from families* about their interactions with schools, neighborhood, and other institutions;
- *Uncover the strategies and processes* families were using as they navigated these multiple systems;
- *Contextualize the school*, situating it as one of the multiple contexts with which youth and their families interacted;
- *Value the expertise and knowledge of community members*, honoring their cultural and social capital as central to the processes of supporting families and schools.

We began our work in the Step-Up partnership with the recognition of the situated and constructed sites of the school and community and the everyday lives of our participants. In 2012, East High had approximately 1,700 students in grades 7–12. The graduation rate was below 40%, and there were reports (discussed above) that for African American and Latino males, the four-year graduation rate was below 10% (Beaudry, 2015). Our access to youth and families was constrained by several factors. Of the 79 youth in the program, only 31 families had provided consent for the school to share their contact information with the NEAD team. The families spanned most of the zip codes within the "crescent" of our city, identified as the neighborhoods with the highest rates of concentrated and extreme poverty (NEAD, 2013). We received 31 names, 29 had working phones and current addresses, 19 consented to have our home visits audio-recorded. By the end of the six months, five families had moved within the city, two had left the city, and several had changed their phone numbers so that we could no longer contact them. The youth attended school and classes sporadically. At the start, it was reported that 49 kids were in 8th and 9th periods (extra time constructed for this program). By March, students reported six to seven kids attending. Because we had walked into a situation that already was not being effective, we knew that within six months we were not going to be able to change the patterns of the youth. In addition, we found that the program itself was not meeting the needs of these students or their families (NEAD, 2013). We were not surprised by the dwindling enrollment.

Our corpus of data included 29 full transcripts of home visits. In addition, our insights from our many visits and phone conversations informed our analysis. As a team, we adopted grounded theory methods of data collection and analysis, looking for salient patterns and themes across transcripts and using our analysis to iteratively shape interviews. We present a sampling of our findings here with the goal of presenting youth and family perspectives on the developmental pathways and trajectories they were engaging with, their goals and expectations, the challenges they faced across contexts, and the strategies and resources they were adopting to work toward their goals. Within each theme, we used the words and insights from different stakeholders and participants, from the parents, youth, and community members.

Goals and Expectations

The first theme focused on *family goals and expectations*. There was a basic goal across most of the families that their child would go to school and graduate along with the basic expectation that the school would support their child along this pathway. Parents and caregivers talked about getting to and finishing school with passion:

> Well, he's going to finish school, if I see it, that's one thing as long as I got breath in my body I'm going to make sure these kids go to school. I don't care what you got to do, crawl there, whatever, you better get in there ... because that's how we was brought up.
>
> *(Interview, 2012)*

Graduating from high school was talked about as a ticket out of poverty, as a pathway to independence, and as a way to help out mom who has worked so hard. For some, the goal was just to pass or just to get a C or D to move on to the next grade. Several parents shared the struggles that not graduating had caused in their own lives: "Your job is all messed up, you know, you don't get the right pay that you're supposed to, you know what I'm saying."

Parents' expectations of the school's Step-Up program included getting smaller classes, tutoring, and other supports. They wanted teachers to demonstrate an understanding of their child's individual education plan (IEP) and specific learning needs. Some viewed the Step-Up program as providing these extra supports, but many were unclear about what actually happened in these extra periods. Parents also expected their children to take responsibility and "step up to the plate": "You could miss school, you're hurting you, you ain't hurting me. I'm trying to get him to see you have to do this for yourself, not for me" (Interview, 2012).

This message was repeated across many families in many different ways. Similar to parents, community members across our research expressed clear goals focused on completing high school, often framed as *"catching up," "getting situated this year,"* and *"moving forward."* During our initial visits, we often aligned these goals with the Step-Up program, in particular attending school and getting to the final two periods of the day. After reviewing transcripts of these visits, we realized that our expectations for youth in these initial messages were woefully low, expressed in terms of "just showing up" or "just making it to class." Referring to what we learned from developing our Interdependence Model, we reframed our goals for both our team and the families to focus on *building relationships*, beginning with seeking understanding of the challenge families were facing and the strategies they were using. We recognized that our role was not to reiterate the school discourse on school achievement—actually this could stand in the way of building trust because we were becoming viewed as only an extension of the school. Instead, we re-positioned ourselves as community members. Our goals for youth also took shape. As we planned family meetings and, with summer approaching, we spent several meetings focused on getting summer jobs for youth. This focus energized our economic and community transformational pathways, and was consistent with our philosophy of interdependence.

Barriers and Challenges

A second theme that emerged as a prevalent challenge for families was *setting and maintaining routines*. Work schedules, hectic lives, and single-parenting presented barriers to getting to school or following through with issues with their child. Parents also cited issues with the school system as challenges. Transportation, frustration getting their children's needs met, and oversight of kids while at school were primary concerns. One father's frustration was clearly expressed:

> Because we're constantly getting phone calls for him and his sister, both of them skipping classes. I just want to know, where the sentries are or where are these kids going. How are they able to leave the school and get somewhere, or be somewhere else besides where they're supposed to be if there's guards and they're supposed to be watched ... You're kind of dependent on the school system as far as teaching them and also keeping an eye, making them try to do the right thing and be in the right spot.
>
> *(Interview, 2012)*

Many other parents echoed these concerns. Parents also recognized challenges they faced with their own children. Just getting their child up in the morning and out of the door was mentioned by several families, as well as the feeling that they have little control—"well, once he gets up out of here I have no idea if he's going or not." Parents received robo-calls when their child was absent, but parents reported that, over time, they ignored them.

For our team of community members and researchers, the barriers and challenges we faced were closely intertwined with our shifting goals and roles within this program. As noted above, as we came to define our goals, we recognized that we wanted to *get the youth re-engaged with school*, but also work toward family engagement with their youth across contexts. This involved challenging the discourses of "underachieving" youth which define success and worth based only on school achievement. It also involved renegotiating our roles as they were defined by both the school and families. As we shifted our goals to building relationships and trust, the primary barrier became time.

Strategies and Processes

A third theme revolved around *strategies and processes* families used to improve outcomes for their family. No parent or caregiver wanted to see their child fail, and in each home, even those with the most challenges, parents provided us with insights into some of the ways they worked toward better outcomes for their child. Parents reported many of the ways they attempted to monitor their children's activities both in school and in the neighborhood, such as insisting that kids come home directly from school. As we shared attendance records with parents, they found it valuable to look at the class-by-class records, to see evidence of the patterns of attendance. Parents expressed the need to know "the details of what is going on" in order to effectively monitor their children's activities.

Many parents also talked about finding alternative programs for their children, recognizing that they were not succeeding in their current context. One mother told us:

> I'm running for everybody, I've got my hands full … but there was like two incidents where an adult put their hands on him twice … And I'm like, okay, there's enough going on with the City School District and the schools … I didn't want to put East High School on the front street like that but it's like I can't take it no more. I don't think it's a good idea that he go there.
>
> *(Interview, 2012)*

Families have found out-of-school programs that they feel provide outlets and additional supports through recreation centers and community agencies. Contrary to the literature on kids living in poverty and not having access to programs outside of school, these programs do exist and a few parents were extremely effective in finding them. Parents also found supports from families and others in their communities. A common strategy involved using older siblings or relatives as role models and mentors.

For youth, one strategy many adopted was disengagement from the school, a strategy that contradicted notions of well-being as associated with succeeding in school. One youth explained clearly why he stopped "showing up":

> Because I'm not there on a regular basis, I'm like maybe a target for a teacher ... and this teacher is supposed to be equipped to handle students like me without degrading me or making me feel like I'm less than human.
>
> *(Interview, 2012)*

Not going had become a strategy to avoid feeling less than human. Alternative developmental trajectories may need to be negotiated and established for some of these youth. The UR Freedom–East program we describe later in this chapter is one attempt to offer alternative trajectories and pathways.

The community also shifted strategies to work toward building relationships and trust. At another level, we strove to reframe some of the discourse that had been adopted around these kids and their families. We encouraged parents to share their goals, their struggles, and their strategies with the school. For the youth who had been labeled "underachieving," we tried to reframe notions of success. We found that we needed to work on school success, but also provide developmental trajectories that included these youth so that we could provide them with possible futures in which they can see themselves.

Step-Up: In the School

NEAD staff and UR team members were also concerned with the kids who were in school but not going to class. The school did not want us to create a program within East, or at the Freedom School. They wanted to have us involved, but team members felt peripheral. NEAD established a team comprised of two staff members, Jeremy and Maurice, to be the intermediaries between the family and the school to reconnect the disconnect that youth and their families felt from school. This team could be in school to give us accurate accounts to share with families and insights into student practices. According to our contract, they were not there to "tutor" because the school was not willing to pay for that.

In spite of the constraints of our contract, the two mentors from Freedom School built positive relationships with the youth. They found out why the kids were not coming to school, and would check in with them and, at times, go to their homes to pick them up. They provided supports to navigate the social systems, such as filling out job applications and finding jobs and navigating community issues, extending relationship building that went way beyond the school context. Again, the Freedom School mentors had the ability and mindset to accept the kids for who they were, never adopting deficit perspectives.

In addition, for many of them, the kids saw the mentors as tied to them, because "their peoples talked highly about Freedom School and NEAD." They knew us. Community connections were being made on the back end to make it more efficient to build trusting relationships with the kids.

We felt that we were doing great work but the goal was so much more than getting the kids to go to extra periods. We were basically "fighting a boxing match without hands" and feeding into the failed systems that the Step-Up program represented. Our research found that how the program was described to families was not what they were actually experiencing in the program. We could not have our names attached to this program because our work depends on the relationships we build and the trust we develop with families. Now that the research team was in full swing and meeting on a weekly basis, we decided together that we no longer felt it was ethical to encourage youth to attend the Step-Up program. We were willing to let the funding go because our relationships with the youth and their families were more important. Even though we were only involved for six months, the strong relationships with families and youth we built continued. One of the kids who wasn't a Step-Up kid, but sat next to one of our kids while Jeremy was there, continued talking with him throughout the program. The Step-Up kid in this class did not come for two months, but Jeremy was there and the young man continued to talk with him. Last year, this young man ended up on our list for the UR Freedom–East program. In the fall of 2015, he and his dad drove their motorcycles over, and enrolled in UR Freedom–East. In February (2017), the young man was passing all of the sections of the Official Readiness Test (ORT) test. He will graduate in June (2017).

UR Freedom–East: Round #3

In 2015, NEAD entered into another collaboration with East High and the University of Rochester to create pathways for youth who were not finding success within our traditional school structures and systems. East High had been designated a failing school, and the University of Rochester entered into an EPO agreement to engage with the school and community on school reform. Joanne had worked with our school district on several initiatives, including a task force on curriculum. When East High was threatened with closure, the Board President reached out to her to explore the possibility of the university serving as the EPO for East High. Joanne connected the Board president with her Dean and a faculty member who was a former Superintendent—they said no … three times. **They persisted.** After many meetings, visits to East, and passionate pleas about being a social justice school of education, the university administration and key faculty members agreed. The partnership took off from that point.

The EPO sought to transform a comprehensive, public, open enrollment urban high school in danger of closing into a model of urban education. In 2014, a leadership team comprised of university faculty and school administrators gathered comprehensive input from a wide variety of stakeholders to develop a full proposal to New York State Department of Education. They met with community agencies (including NEAD), Rochester's mayor, parents, community members, teachers, administrators, and students. More than 2,000 stakeholders over the course of six months provided extensive input, including from approximately 1,200 students across grades 7 to 12 at the school in September 2014. They documented answers to questions about what students would like to see at East, what they thought needed changing, what classes they would like to take, and how the EPO could better involve their families.

After analyzing data gathered from a year and a half of meetings, interviews, and focus groups, the university developed a full proposal that was submitted to the state in December 2014. The university was approved to serve as the EPO, beginning July 1, 2015. The UR East EPO opened the doors to approximately 1,400 students in grades 6 to 12 on September 8, 2015. A key initiative articulated in the EPO was to partner with community-based organizations throughout Rochester to support all East High students, even those who had essentially dropped out.

Constructing UR Freedom–East: "Reconnecting Youth"

NEAD was approached by the new East administration to address the needs of some of the youth within this new partnership who were not finding successful pathways. The initial proposal for UR Freedom–East clearly explicated the philosophical and conceptual perspectives that have intentionally framed all of our youth, family, and community initiatives. The strength-based, community-centric, and culturally relevant approach, grounded in Freedom School practices, challenged the deficit views of youth who many have labeled as "disengaged." These are the youth in our opening story who were told they needed to leave the school, and are too easily put in handcuffs by adults who view them as trouble-makers and thugs. The program narrative represented our perspective:

> It is important to note that youth do not disconnect from traditional developmental pathways because of the failure of any one system. Likewise, *reconnecting* youth requires collaboration and coordination among multiple youth-serving systems. Freedom School has done well to bridge students, and their respective families, to community resources. Respect, credibility, and relationship building are crucial components that are incorporated when Freedom School staff conduct intervention service delivery to RCSD [Rochester City School District] youth and during parent engagement activities. Because Freedom School staff are members of the students' community, their display of investment is beyond a professional obligation; it is a personal mission.
>
> *(East High Freedom School Off-Site Option Proposal, 2015)*

The program we proposed was also grounded in a deep understanding of the "unjust social arrangements" (Ladson-Billings, 1995) that have positioned some of our youth and their families in particular ways. With a fundamental belief that all students are capable of success, a key component of the proposal was building learning communities that offer a sense of safety, love, care, and personal power that lead to transformative education. We also reframed parent engagement. With our commitment to improving outcomes for all students, not just some, we began by meeting families "where they are," building trust and expecting responsibility, and basing interactions on mutual respect. This relational approach was based on a "socially critical, equity-oriented and community minded view of participation" (Smyth, 2009). It contrasts with other parent involvement initiatives that are often manipulative and exploitive in the ways they position parents as passive "clients" of schools rather than as active, equal change agents in the dynamic processes of educating youth to become lifelong learners (Banks, 2007). Our goal was, and continues to be, a community-based model that aims for collective participation (Warren, Hong, Rubin, & Uy, 2009).

We proposed to serve 30 children who had failed 9th grade at least twice, along with their families, through a program focused on credit recovery, building on our success with the East–Freedom Connection and the lessons learned from our involvement with the Step-Up Program. Everyone was aware of the challenges facing our community, families, and youth. We knew it would be difficult to find the students who had been repeating 9th grade and often not coming to school at all. These 17- to 21-year-olds had not experienced success along the traditional school trajectories, but we believed in their potential to succeed in ways that they would come to define as success over time. Our experiences through two years of UR Freedom–East demonstrated multiple challenges, including the processes of re-engaging these youth, the persistent deficit views of these kids, their families and "alternative pathways," and the systemic and structural forces that framed these discourses and perspectives. However, this is also a story of reframing and reclaiming identities, of many successes, and change.

The initial program proposal continued to shift, and through negotiations with East High it was determined that we would work with youth toward their graduate equivalency, or "TASC" (Test Assessing Secondary Completion) diplomas. After we had recruited a core group of students, parents and scholars were invited to a family meeting to learn more about the program, and in particular to catch up with the shifting focus and goals. We discussed program logistics and our goals of getting an equivalency diploma and moving forward with jobs, education, and careers. A parent was determined to see her son "walking the stage at East High" and we understood that these youth, with their diplomas, would be able to walk that stage. After hearing this strongly felt desire about a diploma, East administration reminded the audience that they would not be receiving diplomas but an equivalency. Recognizing the challenges that so many youth face in finishing high school in our district (more than 50%) and the need for alternative pathways for these youth, NEAD staff and then parents began giving testimonials, standing and telling how they had taken different pathways. A staff member told us about getting pregnant young, getting her GED, and then entering college and pursuing a nursing degree. Another community member told of his struggles with finishing high school and how he pursued his GED. A mother then shared her story. One by one, the adults and mentors in this room spoke directly to the youth, telling them that they were not diminished by taking an alternative pathway. In fact, they were strong.

Alternative Spaces Reframing Youth Engagement, Belonging, and Identities

UR Freedom–East thus emerged as an "alternative education program" to specifically address the youth from East High who had chosen, or been counseled into, this alternative pathway. Youth told us that they came to this program because they were stuck in 9th grade with few or no credits (feeling too old to attend classes with 15-year-olds), they were mandated to come by their parole officers, or they had stopped going to classes or attending school at all.

The words of youth, community activists, and university co-researchers during team meetings and through informal conversations provided a glimpse into the transformative space that has been co-constructed at the Freedom School. Our work and analysis of data (iteratively generated) builds on the literature on alternative school programs designed to re-engage "disengaged" youth (e.g. McGregor & Mills, 2011, 2012; Tyler & Lofstrum, 2009). Although much literature supports such contexts as "viable alternatives," researchers also express concern that such programs may foster inequality and injustice by providing means for the mainstream sector to "abrogate their responsivity to vulnerable young people in their care" (McGregor & Mills, 2011, p. 20). We approached our work with these cautions in mind as we continue to explore how youth in our community are being positioned as disengaged and less-valued, and how they and the community are pushing back.

We also expanded our theoretical framework as we considered the identity work taking shape. Social practice theories of identities and sociocultural frameworks of positioning informed our analysis of data and our practice as educators and community members. At UR Freedom–East, the hybrid space constructed, where youth were navigating between being disengaged and engaged, between being East students and members of the Freedom School community and family, between being students and active community participants, became more intentional and explicit over time. We directed our attention to exploring and understanding the complex interactions between youth, leaders, activists, and community and the generative potential of these "contested spaces" (Holland &

Lave, 2009) for creating not only alternative places of learning but also novel identities and alternative pathways for our scholars.

Holland and Leander (2004) encouraged researchers to explore how subjectivities are created by experiences of being positioned. In more recent work, Holland and Lave (2009) direct our attention to the relationship between social, political, and economic struggles and the practices and subjectivities they produce. In particular, they explore how long-term struggles relate to contentious local practices and how they are enacted in specific ways in local contexts. Simultaneously, they situated these struggles between local and cultural politics, connecting the local and translocal and the "unfinished character of history-in-person" (p. 14). These frameworks also align with our broader goals of school reform and urban transformation. As such, we explore the possibilities of "self-authoring" (Holland & Leander, 2004, p. 136), but recognize how social categories such as "troubled youth" are constructed within regimes of power and knowledge. Our opening story illustrated that it is difficult to engage in the work of self-authoring when you are being put in handcuffs.

Emerging Themes: Pushing Back

Consistent with our practice as co-researchers and co-implementers, as we worked to develop the UR Freedom–East program and spaces for these youth, we engaged in iterative cycles of data collection–analysis–implementation–collection to build our local evidence base. Our youth, community researchers, and university team members participated in the Freedom Cafe in regular research team meetings. Through analysis of the words of all participants, we uncovered generative frictions between ways youth were being positioned, and the ways they were "pushing back" (Figure 6.1). Youth described the ways they were constantly being positioned by institutions, police officers, and others as criminals, as disengaged, and as not belonging. But they were pushing back against being viewed and treated as less-valued. This process was enacted through reconceptualizing engagement, reframing themselves as community members in their program and beyond, and co-constructing novel agentive selves who can

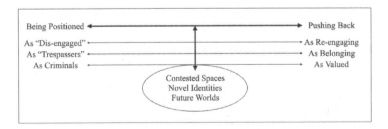

FIGURE 6.1 Tensions, pathways, and spaces

make a difference in their world. We found these frictions being enacted in the unique and contested spaces of UR Freedom–East, this unique alternative school program, and across their communities. In the next section of this chapter, we present data on the generative frictions we have identified.

From Dis-engaged to Re-engaging

Two primary reasons youth were referred to UR Freedom–East were poor attendance and no longer being enrolled. Our youth affirmed they came to Freedom School because of "not going to school, skipping class" and being chronically late. One young woman had not gone to school for two years, another reported she had been in school "17 times out of the whole year." For others, they had no choice, "it's either I come here or I go to jail." One young man captured his feelings of disengagement, but also reconnecting, in a spontaneous spoken word:

> It's like living in hell in a cage, is it all forgiven or is it the same page …
> Can't break out of the bubble, feels like everything I say is mumble, everyone stumbles.
> Take a walk in my shoes, I've been abused …
> I can feel it in my fingertips slipping, but I've got a firm grip
> *(Spoken word poem, 8/2015)*

A prevalent cause reported for students' disengagement came from feeling like teachers did not seem to care. One young woman said "I've been to four high schools and I can count on my fingers and toes teachers that told me you can do what you want to do because as long as you show up, I'm getting paid." They expressed being "set up for failure." Others defended the teachers, and listed other potential reasons including gang violence, being jumped, and the neighborhood. At our final focus group of the first year, the youth represented themselves as re-engaging. Several young men and women had young children of their own, many of our youth were living between multiple homes, and by the end of program, most of them had jobs. A teacher summarized: "Now I understand where you come from, what you go through … what's going on when you ain't in school." The youth overwhelmingly expressed relationships with the adults and the deep level of care at Freedom School as the key to re-engaging. One young man summed it up: "They put love."

From "Trespassers/Criminals" to Belonging as Community Members

To enroll in UR Freedom–East, students who were not enrolled at East High School first needed to re-enroll; those that were still on East's roster needed to let the administrator or a counselor know they were interested in this program. Where they belonged and where they were welcomed became contested during the year. Our leaders were told not to bring "those boys" to East High. The Freedom School teachers pushed back. They noted "the portrayal of kids in our community is not what you find when you actually interact with them." They also noted the challenges of "bridging the disconnect," the preconceived notions that many adults have when meeting or working with "our" kids. Our youth pushed back in several ways as well. Perhaps the most effective was refusing to accept the boundaries being constructed or the position of not belonging. They viewed themselves as belonging more broadly; taking care of family, and helping to build their community.

Bringing It Together

In the contested spaces between the EPO and UR Freedom–East, between the community and school, and within our research team meetings, we found evidence of youth "pushing back" against dominant discourses that positioned them as disengaged, as "trespassers," and as criminals. These generative frictions produced the co-construction and re-framing of their identities as engaged scholars and valued community members. At our first team meeting, one young man told us he wanted to do demolition work to "get my anger out, breaking stuff." In our final focus group, he expressed wanting to become an architect. This shift in identities, in possible selves, represents the enduring potential of this program well beyond "GED prep." This research has the potential to help us understand how we can move from perceptions of "less-valued" youth to recognizing the generative potential of these contested spaces for creating alternative places of learning, but also new identities and alternative pathways for our youth.

Although the Schott Report exaggerated Rochester's failure to meet the educational needs of our youth, our current graduation rates demonstrate the work we still have ahead of us. In the 2016 cohort in the City of Rochester, the four-year graduation rate for the school district in general was 48%, with 34% receiving a Regents Diploma, 5% earning Regents with advanced designation, and 9% local diplomas for students with disabilities. We had 26% of students still enrolled, and 24% dropping out.[2] Our work across eight years with the youth who are not succeeding in our schools clearly demonstrated that we can create spaces and pathways for these kids to succeed. We summarize how our collaborations can provide insights into how to reframe narratives and reposition these youth, how to create spaces for novel identities and new pathways to take shape, and the processes and practices that continue to create barriers to serving our children and families. We end by making the case for recentering CBOs in our work with schools, as we connect the multiple hubs across our community and activate pathways for sustainable transformation.

We are constantly challenged by measures of success. This became evident in our work with the Step-Up families, when we initially found ourselves aligning with the school rhetoric of "showing up." When we realigned our goals with our principles, conversing with families and youth about goals, barriers, and strategies, we built authentic relationships. Records of attendance, of just showing up, are counted as success as well. However, together with the youth we created high expectations of getting a degree, getting a job, and becoming active members of their community.

Positioning and Repositioning

Through our team's ongoing analysis and processes of abduction, we had been exploring theories of positioning as we thought about our work with the kids at UR Freedom–East. A team member pointed out, we used to talk about roles, but "positioning is a different theory because you can change it." The narratives of urban youth discussed at the beginning of this chapter are hegemonic, and we found them woven into our interactions with schools and other institutions across the hubs in our model.

A key question raised by our team centers around the basic disconnect that frames many of these incidences and conversations. A team member noted:

> What happens if the image Eye News, television, media is portraying our kids in a certain way and the people who have been assigned or credentialed to work with them have never had any other interaction with them than the way they've been portrayed in these platforms? How do you bridge the disconnect?
>
> *(Team meeting, 2016)*

He continued, "this speaks to something that is overarching in our community. The portrayal of kids from our community is not what you find when you actually interact with them." Across our programs we have documented the strengths and potential of kids who many have written off. A community member frames how this begins with a mindset of service and caring:

> Each one of these people [who are positioning these kids as not succeeding, as disengaged] have never really sat down and engaged any one of these kids in their own environment. You know, I'm just going to listen, I ain't going to say a word. Tell me whatever you want to tell me, I ain't going to judge you. I'm just going to hear.
>
> *(Interview, 2016)*

And what we hear is youth developing powerful counter-narratives as they position themselves as successful, strong, and proud.

Informing Our Model of Transformational Pathways for Youth

Our collaborations with East High school provide evidence of the need to work toward systematic and sustained approaches to family–school–community partnerships (Weiss et al., 2010). We argue that we need to re-center community members and families in initiatives that focus on our children's education and well-being. Community members serve as valuable leaders in building sustainable collaborations that take into account local ecologies and practices and enhance access to resources and increased social capital for youth and families. As primary mediators and moderators of neighborhood effects, the strategies and processes families adopt need to be understood so that we can support those that are leading to positive outcomes and local ways of "becoming."

Our approach expands our model of interdependent processes and transformational pathways to include schools in partnerships. The developmental processes we identified first in the Freedom Market and then across hubs in our community are intentionally interwoven in the practices guiding UR Freedom–East (building relationships, building community, being family, communicating, belonging and becoming). The cultural, social, educational, economic, political, and research transformational pathways are also activated in this context through intentional engagement of all stakeholders. Through these processes and pathways, our approach challenges the dominant deficit discourses of inequality and disengagement, and the unjust social arrangements framing these discourses, shifting to perspectives and practices that recognize the potential of families and scholars to build and mobilize resources, construct social, educational and political pathways, and transform their communities and their futures.

As we consider collaborations in both research and community initiatives, we take up Lawson's (2003) challenge to question the institutional aims of collaborative work. She asks, "Is the aim to fortify and maintain existing institutions? Or is the aim to transform and create new ones?" (p. 46). We learned that we must work toward transformation in the schools, to challenge the deficit discourse about disengaged families and youth and work toward reconceptualizing stakeholder goals and expectations. In addition, we must challenge our practices in building collaborations—to ensure time to build relationships and trust, to create a model that puts community knowledge and resources at its center and works toward co-constructing successful developmental pathways for youth.

We end by sharing what we've learned from the many years of creating alternative spaces for youth. As stated above, reconnecting these youth and crafting alternative pathways for youth is beyond a professional obligation for Freedom School staff, it is a personal mission. The Freedom Schools model, with a mindset of service, caring, and community, frames every action and interaction in these programs. We also bring our emerging understanding of the importance of space. The space we've created is unique, with foundations in rhizomatic structures and practices of dissensus (Chapter 3). We intentionally construct contested spaces where multiple perspectives, agendas, narratives, histories, and identities collide.

Coda

In early February 2017, UR Freedom–East youth were taking their ORT—the test to determine if they are ready to take the TASC. Over their lunch in the Freedom Café, four youth sat and discussed the test. They shared the ways they addressed questions, the items they felt good about, and those that they found challenging. When she came to our program, one young woman had been described as disconnected and introverted at East High. They used to "lose" her because she would hide at school (literally under the stairs) rather than going to class. She was described as being depressed and rarely interacted with others. This same girl, now more of a young woman, told her peers that she thought the test was fun, especially the math. She was passing every section with high scores, and was almost ready to take the TASC. And another young woman, a mom of a one-year-old, was at East High but was considered "over age and under credit." The school determined that she wasn't attending classes enough to be able be done by the end of June. She had 11 credits, but she was not going to school, partly because she could not bring her son with her. On the two days of testing, she passed her entire first round of tests. She wants to be a forensic pathologist, and is now living with her boyfriend and sharing care for their child. These young adults are succeeding as learners and students, and they know it. They are exhausted from studying and two days of testing, but they are proud.

Notes

1 Available at http://blackboysreport.org/.
2 Data sourced from https://data.nysed.gov, 2016.

References

Banks, J.A. (2007). *Learning in and out of school in diverse environments: Life-long, life-wide, life-deep*. The LIFE Center and Center for Multicultural Education, University of Washington.

Beaudry, A. (ed.) (2015). *Black lives matter: The Schott 50 state report on public education and Black males*. The Metropolitan Center for Research on Equity and the Transformation of Schools at New York University. Retrieved from: http://blackboysreport.org.

Burton, L.M. & Jarrett, R.L. (2000). In the mix, yet on the margins: The place of families in urban neighborhood and child development research. *Journal of Marriage and Family, 62*(4), 1114–1135.

Emerson, L., Fear, J., Fox, S., & Sanders, E. (2012). *Parental engagement in learning and schooling: Lessons from research*. A report by the Australian Research Alliance for Children and Youth (ARACY) for the Family-School and Community Partnerships Bureau.

Furstenberg. F.F., Cook, T.D., Eccles, J., Elder, G.H., & Sameroff, A. (1999). *Managing to make it: Urban families and adolescent success*. Chicago, IL: University of Chicago Press.

Groenke, S.L., Haddix, M., Glenn, W.J., Kirkland, D.E., Price-Dennis, D., & Coleman-King, C. (2015). Disrupting and dismantling the dominant vision of youth of color. *English Journal, 104*(3), 35–40.

Harper, S.R. (2015). Success in these schools? Visual counternarratives of young men of color and urban high schools they attend. *Urban Education, 50*(2), 139–169.

Holland, D. & Lave, J. (2009). Social practice theory and the historical production of persons. *Actio: An International Journal of Human Activity Theory, 2*, 1–15.

Holland, D. & Leander, K. (2004). Ethnographic studies of positioning and subjectivity. *Ethos, 32*(2), 127–139.

Kinloch, V. (2007). The "White-ification of the hood": Power, politics, and youth performing narratives of community. *Language Arts, 85*(1), 61–68.

Ladson-Billings, G. (1995). Toward a theory of culturally relevant pedagogy. *American Educational Research Journal, 32*(3), 465–491.

Lawson, H.A. (2003). Pursuing and securing collaboration to improve results. *Yearbook of the National Society for the Study of Education, 102*(2), 45–73.

Leventhal, T. & Brooks-Gunn, J. (2000). The neighborhoods they live in: The effects of neighborhood residence on child and adolescent outcomes. *Psychological Bulletin, 126*(2), 309–337.

McGregor, G. & Mills, M. (2012). Alternative education sites and marginalized young people: "I wish there were more schools like this one." *International Journal of Inclusive Education, 16*(8), 843–862.

McGregor, G. & Mills, M. (2011). Sketching alternative visions of schooling. *Social Alternatives, 30*(4), 20–24.

NEAD (2013). *Family Engagement Report*, East High–North East Area Development (NEAD) Collaboration December 2012–May 2013.

NYSED (2015). New York State school report card data. Retrieved from https://data.nysed.gov/reportcard.php?year=2015.

Smyth, J. (2009). Critically engaged community capacity building and the "community organizing" approach in disadvantaged contexts. *Critical Studies in Education, 50*(1), 9–22. DOI:10.1080/17508480802526629.

Tyler, J.H. & Lofstrom, M. (2009). Finishing high school: Alternative pathways and dropout recovery. *Future of Children, 18*(1), 77–103.

Warren, M.R., Hong, S., Rubin, C.L., & Uy, P.S. (2009). Beyond the bake sale: A community-based relational approach to parent engagement in schools. *Teachers College Record, 111*(9), 2209–2254.

Weiss, H.B., Lopez, M.E., & Rosenberg, H. (December 2010). *Beyond random acts: Family, school, community engagements as an integral part of education reform*. The National Policy Forum for Family, School, & Community Engagement. Cambridge, MA: Harvard Family Research Project and SEDL.

7

DOING DOUBLE DUTCH

Rhythms of Transformation Across and Within the Community

Joyce Duckles, George Moses, Ryan Van Alstyne

> Rhythm is the soul of life. The whole universe revolves in rhythm. Everything and every human action revolves in rhythm.
>
> —*Babatunde Olatunji*

As we end the story of our collaboration in this chapter, we share with you our evolution and an emerging node in our model. Parents who had connected with us through our other nodes—the reconstructed Market, the Freedom School, and the murals—came together around the goal of creating access to fresh foods for families in the community. Some parents were long-time activists, others were involved in parent advocacy, and others had not previously been involved and expressed doubts about their ability to contribute. Over two years, this grassroots group met in the Parent Room at a local elementary school, another hub we had uncovered that already embodied many of our processes and pathways. It has grown to become the Beechwood Greenhouse Collaborative, a new node in the Interdependence Model, with plans to build greenhouses, gardens, and gathering spaces to support sustainable change in Beechwood.

As new community initiatives and hubs emerge, we are recognizing the value of "having the doors open," particularly for those who had felt marginalized or peripheral to the changes taking place in the neighborhood. We came back to our primary process of building relationships, recognizing that this is a "pathway in" to engagement with community and the foundation of transformation. Our model was expanding with more hubs, and as a team we found that the model that we had developed through our research was now informing our practices, making the work of urban transformation intentional.

As we discussed the pathways in, and the pathways between hubs in our model, we began to question the way we were representing the model. How

Doing Double Dutch 105

do we explore pathways in, the movement towards transformation of the community, and trajectories through and beyond? As a research team member noted, "we are not a closed system, we're open." We revisited our model of hubs and pathways at a research team meeting:

Joyce: It looks like it's closed. It looks static. We need arrows coming in and coming out as well, just to signify it's an open system. How do we make sure that the door is open?

Robert: Have you ever done Double Dutch?

Joyce: Yeah.

Robert: Yeah? So that's what this reminds me of, like, these circles are constantly moving, right? Like the matrix. And then you Double Dutch on the side, until you decide to jump into one of these pathways. Whether it's the Market, the school, university, School 33, you know, you just Double Dutch. Then you jump in, you slide, and there you go. And you can swirl around any one of these hubs.

Joyce: That's a really great metaphor, because Double Dutch, you gotta get the rhythm first.

George: Right, cause if you don't get the rhythm you can't actually get in. So let's talk about the rhythm of getting in.

Joyce: And your first couple of tries it doesn't work [everyone laughing]. But you get better at it.

Joel: And you can't get in and be stagnant, you have to, once you're in, be part of it.

Joyce: And you can never do it alone. You need at least two others, right?

(Team meeting, 3/2016)

FIGURE 7.1 Team concept map of connections

We continued to add emerging hubs to our diagram, mapping relationships and connections (see Figure 7.1). The conversation continued into concepts of dynamism and movement, synergy and energy:

Maurice: It always feels very dynamic.
Wallace: The first law of thermodynamics is what? Energy and matter do not disappear. It transforms. Energy never disappears. Matter never disappears. It transforms into other matter, other forms. You can't destroy it. It transforms.

(Research team meeting 2/2015)

Rhythms, Pathways and Spaces: Expanding Understandings of Community Transformation

The Double Dutch metaphor embodied the dynamism, rhythms and energy that we had all been experiencing and thinking about as we navigated the many hubs across Beechwood (Green, 2014). Our analytic attention had been turning toward the boundaries and spaces between the hubs. Educational researchers and activists engaged in participatory ethnography with an emancipatory vision (Kinloch, Larson, Faulstich Orellana, & Lewis, 2016) interested in community transformation have demonstrated increased attention to the generative potential of boundaries as spaces of learning and change. In particular, many scholars have stressed the learning potential of boundary crossing (Akkerman, 2011; Akkerman & Bakker, 2011). Cultural-historical theorists have explored the changing nature of participation over time and across dynamic communities (Gutiérrez & Rogoff, 2003) and horizontal learning systems (Engeström, 2001). Boundary crossing has been proposed as a way to introduce new ways of participating in established practices as well as expanding and transforming these practices (Akkerman, 2011). This analytic lens can lead researchers to examine how people "traverse or otherwise connect one environment with another in their everyday lives" and how opportunities to learn are "organized and accomplished through trajectories connecting multiple places" (Leander, Phillips, & Taylor, 2010, p. 331).

Trajectories also imply movement and energy. Leander et al. (2010) apply the metaphors of houses from the critical geography work of Lefebvre (1991) and rhizomes from Deleuze and Guattari (1987) to emphasize the "continual movements and transformations" and connections across places and within spaces (p. 341). Although a house may appear as a stable physical structure, it is actually a nexus of in and out conduits through which energy flows, just as social spaces are produced through energy and movement. Lefebvre encourages us to increase our sensitivities to movement and the "diverse, multiple rhythms of everyday life" (2004, p. 20). In a similar way, rhizomes are connected yet open systems through which nutrients flow. With underground systems of shoots, roots, and nodes, they mirror the ways surface entities that appear distinct have subterranean connections. Throughout our work, we have adopted the rhizome metaphor to illustrate the generative, yet often hidden, energies and capacities across spaces.

As activists and co-researchers, our overarching goal is to understand relationships and social pathways within and across the hubs we have identified in the neighborhood that are leading to authentic and meaningful change. In this chapter, we present our most recent analytic attention to pathways and spaces, movement and rhythms, and the generative potential of boundary crossing. We adopt the metaphor of "doing Double Dutch" and develop themes of "pathways in" as opening doors, "pathways through" as feeling the rhythms, and the learning and dexterity that energizes trajectories beyond the hubs in our neighborhood. We propose the constructs of rhythm, attunement, and dexterity as conceptual and analytic tools to inform our understanding of pathways and boundaries as "hidden energies" for learning and community transformation.

Opening Doors—Pathways In

Nespor (2006) directs researchers to "note how both people and things change as they move through networks that mesh at some points and generate tensions at others" (p. 301). As we look at what moves, Nespor (2006) recommends challenging the boundaries and looking at how neighborhoods are defined by the intersections of multiple pathways.

As we developed our model of interdependent hubs, our initial concept maps depicted the hubs and pathways but it had the appearance of a closed system. We had focused on the processes and activities, but, as Nespor (2006) notes, we were challenged in seeing the movement and, in particular, the movement in and out. In the store and across hubs, we recognized the challenge of engaging community members who have traditionally been "disengaged," directing our attention to "pathways in." Our data suggested that this begins with meeting people "where they're at" and not judging others:

> I think it's more like, how do we go about reaching the people without it, without them getting offensive. To you talking to them, and then, meeting them where they're at. Trying to find out what's going on, to just not always being judgmental.
> *(Greenhouse Collaborative Meeting, 2/2015)*

We realized that as community activists we needed to attend to what "meeting people where they're at" looks like, and how it can be facilitated. As we were analyzing data, a co-researcher suggested that it begins with opening the doors wider:

> So when we were talking about the guys on the street corners and the dealers and stuff, but making pathways available for them as well? You

can't judge them because that's where they are right now, but instead you have to connect with them and have pathways for them … And some of them won't. We may not get all of them, but if we get one or two to come along we're making progress. So, that's harder work, going from feeling totally disengaged to entering the work that you want to do. How do we pull them along or at least make pathways for them? Cause it can't always be them that are there and ready to move. Sometimes you've got to make the door wider open some way or another.

(Team meeting, 9/2015)

Parents and community developers talked often of making pathways for everyone who "wants to come along" and opening the doors in intentional ways. Our data have many examples of an apprenticeship model across hubs with attention to providing first-time experiences to youth and adults. Through the Work Experience Program (WEP), adults have come to work in the Market, the NEAD office, and the Freedom School Café. Youth are also trained at the Market and as "junior servant leaders" in the Freedom School. A community member described these interactions as "reshaping what interactions look like in the community." Processes of building relationships and ways of interacting echo across the hubs—the consistency is intentional. Rather than accepting silos, the connections between spaces ensure the consistencies as individuals move along the pathways.

This means that "pathways in" can occur through any hub. At a team meeting, a co-researcher pointed to the lines we were drawing between hubs on our concept map:

That's what I would say about these lines. It's intentional. It's organic but it's intentional. It's intentional for them to come to any one of these hubs and to be able to organically, to be exposed to each of them.

(Team meeting, 9/2015)

Several years later, this was articulated through the Double Dutch metaphor. We recognized the circles or hubs as constantly moving. And then:

you Double Dutch on the side, until you decide to jump into one of these pathways. Whether it's the market, the school, university, or garden, you know, you just Double Dutch. Then you jump in, you slide, and there you go.

Feeling the Rhythms—Pathways Through and Between Hubs

Opening the doors is the beginning. A co-researcher described how participants enter on pathways through and between the hubs. It begins with listening and using ideas shared by residents:

So that they know, hey, I am relevant, I am important, I am a part of it. Then through that, it allows them to spread the word or the message to others. But when you don't make them feel welcome, you don't make them feel like their voices are heard, they're going to continue down the same roads that they've been. It's just the bottom line.

(Team meeting, 10/2015)

Feeling the rhythms means feeling part of something bigger. A team member described this as people "becoming conscious or aware and feeling, you know I'm a part, because the conversations that we now have, they participate in, where before they didn't" (Team meeting, 10/2015). They are now "at the table." They are part of the "Freedom Movement."

The Double Dutch metaphor becomes powerful here for illustrating the challenges of feeling the rhythms across hubs. The Double Dutch conversation continued in our meeting, focusing on "getting the rhythm" so that you can jump in. We noted that you get better at "jumping in" over time, that you can't be "stagnant" because, once you're in, you have to be a part of it. NEAD's director asked if we all knew how to "twirl," noting that everyone can't jump in, but most people know how to twirl. He extended it further:

So that metaphor is, you just, what you're doing is you get into rhythm. So as we start to talk about energy it's attunement. Cause we're using static in different ways—static being still or static where tuning in stations. So you're tuning until you get to the right station. So it's energy. So what you're trying to do is get on the right energy level … so that's Double Dutch. You have that pathway to get in, but you have to Double Dutch to get in, and once you get in you have to have the right energy to get in rhythm with everything else.

(Team meeting, 10/2015)

The pathways through and between are also co-constructed in intentional ways. In our early renditions of our model, we began to recognize the hubs and the consistency of processes within them. We spoke of "challenging the norms" that have come to be accepted in the community by building rhizomatic connections between spaces that echo similar messages, practices, and expectations. Again, the rhythms of different hubs were noticed:

All components at some point tie in on a different level, whether it be social, economical, health, educational … so there's like a constant interjection between them. So even though it may look static-y, it may be static, but at any frequency there's always going to be static until you fine tune it. It's the fine tuning of all the components together that makes you come to a strong frequency to push out there.

(Team meeting, 9/2015)

Pushing "out there" means moving beyond, extending the movement beyond the neighborhood.

Our students from UR Freedom–East are also following these pathways. Their "pathways in" have often been circuitous. As they noted in Chapter 6, some came to this program because the school referred them, some found us through friends, and others were mandated by the courts. When they began, they were unsure of their abilities to succeed, to earn their equivalency diplomas, and to move beyond to find employment and careers.

Sharing the Rhythm and Developing Dexterity—Pathways Beyond

Part of moving forward is sharing the rhythm and "passing it forward": "You reach one, you teach them, and then you let them reach someone else." Keeping up the momentum and sharing the rhythm is described as central to the "Freedom Movement." This was illustrated during a team meeting using our model of rhizomes:

Unknown: I know irises grow in a rhizome and that's how they spread. I mean I don't know if this is an issue, but after a while if you don't cut them up and replant them the center will die.
Joanne: So what does that mean for our data?
Joyce: Well, you're never going to stop, you have to keep changing and developing and if you've got entrepreneurial ventures that become their own nodes, they are building on the same principles, same processes that we've been talking about, and then they move to another community.
George: Yeah, and what does that mean for this work?
Joanne: So they can become centers of their own.
George: There you go.

(Team meeting, 4/2013)

Another "pathway beyond" takes shape through developing the skills or the "dexterity" to enter different spaces with different rhythms. Stories of community residents who are "making it" are shared often. Abby began as a WEP worker in the store. She worked in the café and received her ServSafe Food Safety certification, and she now has a job downtown. One researcher noted that Abby could have kept working her WEP hours, but "now she's in the mindset of I want something of my own." Community members, both adults and children, navigate the multiple rhythms of the different hubs in the community, learning how to "jump in" and participate. Similar to the repertoires for participating in practices proposed by Gutiérrez and Rogoff (2003), we can encourage people "to develop dexterity in determining which approach from their repertoire is appropriate under which circumstances" (p. 22) or across varying activity settings. We propose that following participants like Abby can add to our understanding of "how engagement in shared and dynamic practices of different communities contributes to individual learning and development" (p. 21). We also argue that developing this dexterity is part of the learning that can empower people to design their own social futures.

Within our research team, we also became aware of how work at boundaries generates learning. Akkerman and Bakker (2011) identified transformation as a recognized mechanism for constituting the learning potential of boundary crossing. In this framework, moving or transgressing from expected roles or modes of interpretation can open up spaces for the construction of new ways of being and thinking. In our roles as university and community researchers, we entered this emergent zone of contact and this joint work at the boundaries. We use the concept of dissensus (Ziarek, 2001) to illuminate the ways that collaborative research can foster generative tensions at the boundaries. A doctoral student on our research team summarized this tension in a memo:

> We do create shared narratives. We also embrace the continuous joint work we are crafting at the boundaries—our unique frameworks, experiences, identities, and practices shape the dialogic spaces we co-construct; lead us to embrace dissensus and recognize the generative potential it holds for us as a research team.
>
> *(Memo, 5/2012)*

Whether in the store or in our team meetings, friction and dissensus emerging from boundaries ground our "constant move forward." As we work together toward urban transformation, stagnation is not an option.

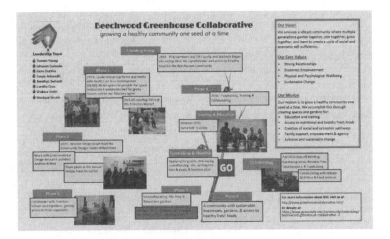

FIGURE 7.2 Phases of the Beechwood Greenhouse Collaborative

As a Representation of Pathways and Trajectories

Creating pathways in, and activating pathways, making connections across space means connecting and engaging residents; moving toward finding rhythms that may vary but have the same, underlying beat. When we all recognize and feel this rhythm, we are moving toward a coordinated movement and collective efficacy.

Research has demonstrated the potential of collective efficacy for driving community transformation (Collins, Neal, & Neal, 2014). Collective efficacy is defined as "residents' perceived collective capacity to take coordinated and independent action on issues that affect neighborhoods" (p. 328). At group and individual levels, collective efficacy has been associated with health and social benefits, including reductions in violent crimes (Browning, Dietz, & Feinberg, 2004), homicide (Morenoff, Sampson, & Raudenbush, 2001), obesity rates (Cohen, Finch, Bower, & Sastry, 2006), and, at the individual level, improvements in self-rated physical health (Browning & Cagney, 2002).

As we consider movement within and across community, we recognize the potential of creating momentum to drive transformation and change. Intentionally connecting hubs involves intentionally connecting residents. Work on Comprehensive Community Initiatives (CCIs) and relational organizing methods demonstrate the power of engaging residents in community change efforts. Collins et al. (2014) propose that "relationally-based community organizing strategies may be effective ways for community organizers to help communities enhance their collective capacity to influence their environment" (p. 334).

We are also adopting a relational perspective, one that views engagement as actively engaging with others, with communities, and with institutions, especially those that sustain poverty and inequalities. We are building on Smyth's (2009) view of engagement as "predicated on a socially activist, collectivist, socially critical, equity-oriented, and community-minded view of participation" (p. 17).

Methodological Challenges

As researchers, the focus on movement and change represents particularly unique methodological challenges. Nespor (2006) describes the work of researchers and ethnographers as looking for patterns. He conceptualizes patterns as "descriptions of processes and networks through which things are moving and changing" (p. 300). It is, however, not easy to focus on movement. Nespor equates this challenge to navigating a "moving dance-floor (historically shaped and propelled) where dissonant orchestras of social relations battle to define the rhythms" (p. 300). To enter into the moving and shifting spaces and practices, he recommends that we take the advice of Latour (1987) and "follow the movement of things." We are directing our theoretical and research lenses to spaces where practices are in the process of being mutually constituted, where different rhythms are taking shape. He also tells us to pay attention to where things have stabilized: "Where the networks and circuits have contingently stabilized, you can look at their structures (e.g. Burt, 2000; Wellman, 1997) and attend to the flows that sustain them" (p. 301). Stabilization also becomes important.

Threats of Stagnation and Stasis

Our attention to movement has also made us aware of the threats of stagnation. The radical democratic construct of dissensus (Ziarek, 2001) helps us theorize a different boundary crossing; creating spaces to speak across difference and to respectfully challenge differing perspectives of theoreticians and practitioners. This is most evident within our research team, in our daily interactions, where we resist the temptation to insist upon consensus and allow our mutually respected differences to inform authentic debate to energize our research and practices.

We also need to consider cohesion and stasis. We proposed "pathways in" taking shape as opening doors by creating spaces for voices. We argued that the intentional redundancy across hubs was providing multiple entry points. However, we know that some community members do not "feel a part of" the changes under construction in Beechwood. We are also interested in why some may choose to stay out, and the physical and psychological barriers that persist. To us, the environments may appear the same, but the potential constraints on engagement based on past experiences may inhibit access. We must take into account how historically closed doors can challenge simplistic views of access to resources or engagement, especially as we consider pathways into the shifting rhythms of community spaces.

Closing Thoughts

The themes of boundaries, movement, and rhythms have permeated our data from the beginning of this long-term collaborative ethnography. We had adopted the theoretical metaphor of rhizomes (Deleuze & Guattari, 1987) to bring attention to pathways and their transformational potential. However, we had been conceptualizing the interdependent hubs as a closed system of relations. Metaphors of Double Dutch extended our attention to pathways in, through, and beyond, reminding us of the value of conceptualizing these systems as open, dynamic, restorative, and generative. As we all go about our daily personal and professional lives, we carry what we have learned from our research with us. We carry lessons about the importance of building relationships into other research and activism work as we travel various pathways. We continue to find ourselves in each other's spaces and places on a regular basis. Our shifting roles as we engage in change and activism includes Joyce and Joanne moving into policy spaces and community members moving into university spaces. We have been able to work with the university's IRB so that our community research partners have researcher IDs and can serve as sub-investigators.

114 Joyce Duckles, et al.

Our activist understanding that this work is predicated on building trusting relationships shapes our research. From restorative practices, we understand that building relationships includes sustaining them through difficulties, and that ending the relationship is not an option (see Chapter 4). Thus, all work is focused on restoring and sustaining the relationships we build so they can continue and flourish. We know now that our research and activism are mutually constituted as we work toward engaging community members in imagining pathways and creating spaces and places that foster connections across their histories, within their families and neighborhoods, and toward their futures.

The Double Dutch metaphor helped us see the rhythms of our collaborative work as we moved across our lives as researchers and activists. We have learned some lessons we think may help others do the kind of deep community transformation work we have described in this book. To researchers, qualitative and quantitative, who have said they want to do this kind of work with communities but don't know how to start, we suggest learning the rhythms of the community you wish to serve by showing up to and spending time at community events as an entry point to building relationships and earning trust. George describes what he calls the Concentric Circles[1] of Trust (see Figure 7.3) which he uses to decide whom to trust and how much to trust them. The outer circle is for people who are well-intentioned but may not be around for long. The middle circle is for people who can be trusted for

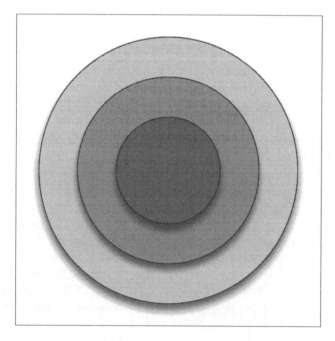

FIGURE 7.3 Concentric circles of trust

the most part, but who may not be able to stand in a crisis. The inner circle is for people who commit for the long haul. All parts of the concentric model are valuable to be sure. Think about which part of the circle you can do. This work takes time; figure out what kind of time you are able to commit as you develop relationships.

For early career faculty, this work can be more difficult given the academy does not reward activist research. We realize you will need to publish in research journals in order to get tenure. You could negotiate with your collaborative community (or school) partners in such publications and let them know you will need some to be sole authored. We also suggest you consider not valuing your work by the numbers the academy uses to value scholarship. For senior faculty, we suggest a continued and forceful challenge to the academy to appropriately value activist work. Community members have asked us, "Why is the university sleeping?" We all need to wake up the academy so that the impact of our research is useful in real time.

Know this work is not for everybody, it is a choice you have to make. We ask you to consider the ethics of working with communities who work against poverty, especially if you are only there to "study them" or build an academic career. You need to ask yourself whether you can sustain the trusting relationships needed for authentic collaborative work with communities. As we look back at the history of the Beechwood neighborhood, we see a trail of well-intentioned researchers with programs and initiatives they believed would make a positive impact. However, when the grant ended, they left. The problems remained and the community was disrupted. For community members living in poverty whose lives are already disrupted and inconsistent, adding inconsistency is simply unethical.

FIGURE 7.4 #FreedomSankofa

Note

1 This is similar to the Convoy Model discussed in Kahn and Antonucci (1980).

References

Akkerman, S.F. (2011). Learning at boundaries. *International Journal of Educational Research*, 50, 21–25. DOI:10.1016/j.ijer.2011.04.005.

Akkerman, S.F. & Bakker, A. (2011). Boundary crossing and boundary objects. *Review of Educational Research*, 81(2), 132–169.

Browning, C.R. & Cagney, K.A. (2002). Neighborhood structural disadvantage, collective efficacy, and self-rated physical health in an urban setting. *Journal of Health and Social Behavior*, 43(4), 383–399.

Browning, C.R., Dietz, R.D., & Feinberg, S.L. (2004). The paradox of social organization: Networks, collective efficacy, and violent crime in urban neighborhoods. *Social Forces*, 83(2), 503–534.

Burt, R.S. (2000). The network structure of social capital. *Research in organizational behavior*, 22, 345–423.

Cohen, D.A., Finch, B.K., Bower, A., & Sastry, N. (2006). Collective efficacy and obesity: The potential influence of social factors on health. *Social Science and Medicine*, 62(3), 769–778.

Collins, C.R., Neal, J.W., & Neal, Z.P. (2014). Transforming individual civic engagement into community collective efficacy: The role of bonding social capital. *American Journal of Community Psychology*, 54(3–4), 328–336.

Deleuze, G. & Guattari, F. (1987). *A thousand plateaus: Capitalism and schizophrenia*. Minneapolis, MN: University of Minnesota Press.

Engeström, Y. (2001). Expansive learning at work: Toward an activity theoretical reconceptualization. *Journal of Education and Work*, 33(1), 133–156.

Green, K. (2014). Doing double dutch methodology: Playing with the practice of participant observer. In D. Paris & M. Winn (Eds.). *Humanizing research: Decolonizing qualitative inquiry with youth and communities* (pp. 147–160). Thousand Oaks, CA: Sage.

Gutiérrez, K. & Rogoff, B. (2003). Cultural ways of learning: Individual traits or repertoires of practice. *Educational Researcher*, 32(5), 19–25.

Kahn, R.L. & Antonucci, T.C. (1980). Convoys over the life course: Attachment, roles, and social support. In P.B. Baltes & O.G. Brim (Eds.), *Life span development and behavior*. Vol. 3 (pp. 253–286). New York, NY: Academic Press.

Kinloch, V., Larson, J., Faulstich Orellana, M., & Lewis, C. (2016). Literacy, equity, and imagination: Researching with/in communities. *Literacy Research: Theory, Method, and Practice*, 1–19. DOI:10.1177/2381336916661541.

Latour, B. (1987). *Science in action*. Cambridge, MA: Harvard University Press.

Leander, K.M., Phillips, N.C., & Taylor, K.H. (2010). The changing social spaces of learning: Mapping new mobilities. *Review of Research in Education*, 34, 329–394. DOI:10.3102/0091732X09358129.

Lefebvre, H. (1991). *The production of space*. D. Nicholson-Smith (Trans.). Oxford: Blackwell.

Lefebvre, H. (2004). *Rhythmanalysis: Space, time and everyday life*. New York, NY: Continuum.

Morenoff, J.D., Sampson, R.J., & Raudenbush, S.W. (2001). Neighborhood inequality, collective efficacy, and the spatial dynamics of urban violence. *Criminology, 39*(3), 517–558.

Nespor, J. (2006). Finding patterns with field notes. In J. Green, C. Camilli, P. Elmore, A. Skukauskaite, & E. Grace (Eds.), *Handbook of complementary methods in educational research* (pp. 297–308). Mahwah, NJ: Lawrence Erlbaum.

Smyth, J. (2009). Critically engaged community capacity building and the "community organizing" approach in disadvantaged contexts. *Critical Studies in Education, 50*(1), 9–22.

Wellman, B. (1997). Structural analysis: From method and metaphor to theory and substance. *Contemporary Studies in Sociology, 15*, 19–61.

Ziarek, E.P. (2001). *An ethics of dissensus: Postmodernity, feminism, and the politics of radical democracy.* Stanford, CA: Stanford University Press.

INDEX

Note: Page numbers for figures appear in *italics*.

#FreedomSankofa 115
1964 riots 9, 11

Abby 110
absenteeism 85, 98
the academy and activist research 49, 115
activism 7–12, 15, 16, 49, 113, 114, 115; and FIGHT 45–6; and murals 32
African Americans 2, 7, 9, 32, 56, 70; 1964 riots 11; population 12; and school graduation 77, 88
agonism 39–40, 50
Akkerman, S.F. 111
Alinsky, Saul 11
"all the way live" day 64, 68–71
Anthony, Susan B. 1, 8, *9*, 9–11
apprenticeship model 108
attunement 107

Bakker, A. 111
banishment 70
becoming 29–30, 101
Beechwood 1, 2, 5, 8, 54, 65–7, 84; population 12
Beechwood Greenhouse Collaborative 104, *111*
being family 27
belonging 29
Berkshire Farms Center and Services for Youth 57, 58

Black lives matter: The Schott 50 state report on public education and black males (Beaudry) 83
Blacks 12; and school graduation 83, 88; *see also* African Americans
Boatwright, Tomás 72, 73
Boldt, G. 22
boundaries 106, 111, 113
boundary crossing 51, 106, 107, 111, 113
brainstorming *17*
breaking bread 42
Breaking Bread (hooks and West) 42
Brooks-Gunn, J. 88
Brooks, Maurice 106
Brown v. *Board of Education* 56
building community 26–7, 33
building relationships 22, 24–5, 33, 41, 77, 101, 104, 108, 113, 114; and Kim 62; and primary pathways to Interdependence Model 61; and researchers working in the store 37; and "Step-Up Program" 90, 92
Burbules, N.C. 6
Burnett, K. 5

Calvin, Brittany 15
CBOs (community-based organizations) 84, 85, 94, 95
child poverty 65
children from Freedom School *55*, 56

Children's Defense Fund (CDF) 56–7
cigarettes 67
Civil Rights Movement 54, 56
co-authoring in the versus 46–7
Cobb, Charles 54, 56
coding 40
cohesion 113
collaborative knowledge-production 48
collaborative writing 46–7
collective efficacy 112
Collins et al. 112
comfort 77
communicating 27–9
community building 26–7, 33
community members, as valuable leaders 101
Comprehensive Community Initiatives (CCIs) 112
concentric circles of trust 114–15
connections 105–6, 108, 112, 114
contested spaces 96–7, 99, 102
conversation 41–3
cooking practices 39
corner store 2, 27–8, 31, 37–8, 43–4, 51, 64; *see also* Freedom Market
criminals, as one identity of youth 99

deaf population 13
de-colonization 46
Deleuze, G. 31, 106
democratic engagements 4
Dempsey, S. 39–40
dexterity 107, 110–11
dialogicality 4, 31, 39
DiFranco, Ani 64
disengagement 98, 107, 108
dissensus 39, 43, 44, 50, 65, 71, 111, 113
Double Dutch metaphor 105, 106, 107, 108, 109, 113, 114
Douglass, Frederick 1, 7–8, 9–10, *10*, 11
drug dealing 56, 64, 69–70
Duckles, Joyce 15, 42, 105, 110
dynamism 106

East Educational Partnership Organization (EPO) 82, 93–4
East–Freedom Connection 84–6, 95
East–Freedom School 84, 85–6
East High School 79–82, 84–96
Eastman Kodak 12
efficacy, collective 112
Emdin, C. 4
energy 106

engaged scholarship 46
engagement 86, 87–8, 91, 112, 113
Engeström, R. 49
Engeström, Y. 49
epistemic injustice 38

family: being 27; engagement 85–6, 87–8, 91; goals and expectations 89–90
Family Nutrition Records 28
fatherhood 44, 45
Father Legacy 44
feminism 43, 44, 45
FIGHT (Fight Independence God Honor Today) 11, 12, 45–6
first-timers 73–6
Flower, L. 3, 5, 7, 41, 48
Food Corps 24–5, 28
food deserts 65–6
food shopping practices 39
Foucault, M. 8, 65
Freedom Market 2, 24–5, 26–31, 32, 55, 65–71, *66*, *67*, *68*; "all the way live" day 64, 68–9; and first-timers 73–6; the stoop 51; and WEP 108
Freedom School Movement 56–62
Freedom School, Rochester 31, 56, 57–8, *59*, 60, 81, 82, 108; men's meetings 45
Freedom Schools model 84, 85, 86, 87, 101
Freedom Summer 56
Freire, P. 46, 62
Fricker, M. 38
frictions 40, 43–6, 50, 71, 73–6, 77, 98, 111; and dissensus 65; with escorting students 81; with youth 99

generative frictions 40, 43–6, 50, 71, 73–6, 98; and dissensus 65; with escorting students 81; with youth 99
graduate equivalency diploma (GED) 95–6
graduation rates 77, 83, 88, 99
Greenwich, Joel Gallegos 16
Groenke et al. 82
grounded theory 40, 47, 89
Guattari, F. 31, 106
Gutiérrez, K.D. 51, 110

Haley Farm 57
Hanny, Courtney 16
Harambee 62

Index

Holland, D. 97
"homeplace" 27
hooks, b. 27, 42
housing development 58
hubs 22, 26, 105, 106, 107, 112, 113; Freedom School 62; and Interdependence Model 23, 46; and pathways 31, 32, 104, 108; and rhythms 109, 110; the store 27, 29, 51; and urban youth 100

identities 96, 97, 99
imani 7
Institutional Review Board (IRB) 42
intentionality 28
Interdependence Model 23–32, 46, 61, 62, 76, 104
Irma 84, 85
Iroquois Nation 8
Ito et al. 6

Jamaican American communities 12
Johnson, Mildred 11

Kajner, T. 38
Karenga, Maulana 7
Kerosuo, H. 49
Kinloch, V. 4, 82
Kodak 8
Kristof, N. 49
kujichagulia 7, 14, 45, 61
kuumba 7, 32
Kwanzaa 7

Larson, Joanne 14, 38, 42, 43, 44, 110; at "all the way live" day 64, 68, 69, 70, 71; standing with the community 72, 73
Latino males, and school graduation 83, 88
Latour, B. 112
Lave, J. 97
Lawson, H.A. 101
Leander et al. 106
Leander, K. 22, 97
Lefebvre, H. 6, 54, 106
Leventhal, T. 88
"Life Lessons at the New 'East–Freedom School'" 84
literacy practices 3–4, 5, 22, 48, 51, 64–5, 65
Liz 85
Lynch, K. 6

Mackey, M. 4–5
march, community 54–6
marginality 27
Market *see* Freedom Market
masculine space 43–4
McClintock, N. 66
McGregor, G. 96
mentors 92–3
Mills, M. 96
Moses, George 14, 38–9, 42, 43, 57, 77, 110; at "all the way live" day 68–9, 70–1; and concentric circles of trust 114; and the Father Legacy 44; and Freedom School 58, 85; on Freedom School men's meetings 45–6; on standing 71–3
Moses, Robert 14, 42, 44, 46, 73–4, 105
movement 106, 107, 113
murals *32*, 32–3
Museum of Kids Art (MOKA) 58

National Policy Forum 87
NEAD (North East Area Development) 2, 56, 57, 58, 62, 65, 69; and East Freedom School 85; purchased Freedom Market 67; and "Step-Up Program" 86, 92; and UR East EPO 93; and UR Freedom–East 84, 94
neighborhood effects 88
Nelson, Kimberly (Kim) 15, 42, 61, 62
Nespor, J. 107, 112–13
New Literacy Studies (NLS) 5
nguzo saba 7, 13, 14, 31, 45, 60–1, 62; and murals 32; and NEAD 57, 58; and UR Freedom–East 84
nia 7
nodes *24*
The North Star 11

Olatunji, Babatunde 104
opening doors 107–8, 113
ORT (Official Readiness Test) 93, 102
outsidedness 27

Page, John 58
Pahl, K. 5
parental involvement 85–6, 95, 104
the park 56
PAR (participatory action research) 40, 47–8

pathways 6, 61, 105, 107, 114; beyond 110–11, 113; in 104, 107–8, 110, 112, 113; through 107, 113; through and between 109; transformational 22–3, 30–1, 32–3, 101–2
patterns 112
Penuel, W.R. 51
place 4–5, 6
pluralist agonism 39
police 11, 69, 70
Polish Americans 12
positioning 100
poverty 65
power disparities 51
power relations 4, 65, 66
public transportation 66
Puerto Ricans 12
pushing back, youth 97–8, 99

race riots 9, 11
reading loss, summer 58
re-engaging 98
Regents Diploma 99
relational organizing methods 112
relational turns 36–8
relationships 106, 107; *see also* building relationships
restorative justice 70, 71–3
rhizomes 20, *21*, 22, 23, 31, 40, 106–7, 110, 113
rhythms 106, 107, 109, 110, 112, 113, 114
Robach, Joe 57
Rochester 7–13, 65, 76–7, 99; *see also* East High School; Freedom School, Rochester
Rochester Area Community Foundation 58
Rochester Freedom School Movement 56–8
Rochester, university 82, 93–4
Rogoff, B. 110
Rommetveit, R. 25
routines, setting and maintaining 90–1
Rowe, D. 22

sankofa 7, 8, 11, 54, 115
sankofa bird 7, 32
school graduation 77, 83, 88, 99
Schott Report 83, 99
self-authoring 97
Seneca Falls 10, 11
Seneca Mothers of the Haudenosaunee 10

Shultz, L. 38
Smalls, TaShara 61–2
Smith, Jeremy 15, 79–80, 81
Smith, Wallace 11, 12, 14–15, 28, 74, 106; at "all the way live" day 64, 68, 69, 70; and first-timers 75, 76
Smyth, J. 112
social action 49; *see also* activism
social pathways 107; *see also* pathways
Soja, E. 6, 54
spaces 4–5, 106, 107, 108, 110, 112, 113, 114; contested 96–7, 99, 102; and Lefebvre 6; and the stoop 51; transactional/transformative 74
spatial rights 54
stabilization 113
stagnation 113
standing with the community 71, 72, 73, 77
Stanton, Elizabeth Cady 9
stasis 113
Step-Up Program 86–93, 95
the stoop *50*, 51
the store *see* corner store
story-behind-the-story 46
struggles, social, political, and economic 97
Student Nonviolent Coordinating Committee (SNCC) 56
success, measures of 100
summer reading loss 58
synergy 106

TASC (Test Assessing Secondary Completion) diplomas 95–6, 102
tobacco 67
trajectories 106, 107; *see also* pathways
transactional/transformative space 74; *see also* spaces
transformational pathways 22–3, 30–1, 32–3, 101–2
transportation 66–7
trespassers 99
trust 41, 42, 92, 101, 114–15
Turkish American communities 12

ujamaa 7, 58
ujima 7, 58
umoja 7, 61
unidirectionality 35, 36, 42
University of Rochester (UR) 82, 93–4
university partnerships 38–40
"urban youth of color" 82–4

UR East EPO 93, 94
UR Freedom–East 84, 94, 98–100, 101, 102, 110
"The Urgency of Now" (Beaudry) 83

Van Alstyne, Ryan 16, 57

Washington, Rose 57
Weiss et al. 87

West, C. 42
Whites 12
women's movement 10–11
Women's Rights Convention 11
Work Experience Program (WEP) 108

youth: apprenticeships 108; of color 82–4; identity 99; and reconnecting 94–6; and repositioning 100